AN OBSESSION WITH
CIGAR BOX
GUITARS

AN Obsession WITH

CIGAR BOX
GUITARS

120 GREAT HAND-BUILT EXAMPLES

DAVID SUTTON

FOX CHAPEL
PUBLISHING

ISBN 978-1-56523-796-4

Library of Congress Cataloging-in-Publication Data

Sutton, David, 1958-
 An obsession with cigar box guitars / David Sutton.
    pages ; cm
 Includes index.
 ISBN 978-1-56523-796-4
 1. Cigar box guitar--Pictorial works. I. Title.
 ML1015.G9S887 2013
 787.87'1920222--dc23
                          2013017300

To learn more about the other great books from Fox Chapel Publishing, or to find a retailer near you, call toll-free 800-457-9112 or visit us at *www.FoxChapelPublishing.com*.

Note to Authors: We are always looking for talented authors to write new books. Please send a brief letter describing your idea to Acquisition Editor, 1970 Broad Street, East Petersburg, PA 17520.

Printed in China
First printing

ACQUISITION EDITOR
Peg Couch

EDITOR
Colleen Dorsey

DEVELOPMENTAL EDITOR
Ayleen Stellhorn

COVER AND INTERIOR DESIGNER
Jason Deller

LAYOUT DESIGNER
Michael Douglas

"Perhaps we're so consumed by our consumer culture that we tend to think of guitars as impossibly complex devices that somebody else has to build. One of the many beauties of the cigar box guitar is that it shatters this myth."

INTRODUCTION

When I tell people about my book, *Cigar Box Guitars*, the conversation often goes like this:

"I wrote a book called *Cigar Box Guitars*."

"What's it about?"

"It's about (dramatic pause) cigar box guitars."

"What's a cigar box guitar?"

**"It's a guitar. Made from…
 a cigar box. You make it yourself."**

Puzzled stare.
"How many strings does a cigar box guitar have?"

"It depends on how many you put on it."

Again, the puzzled stare.

Really now. What is a cigar box guitar?

A cigar box guitar is a simple stringed instrument that you build yourself, usually by poking a dowel, board, or stick through a discarded wooden cigar box and then outfitting it with guitar strings. For a lot of builders and enthusiasts, the cigar box guitar then becomes a point of departure to begin making music.

Even at this stage, some people still give me that puzzled look. Perhaps we're so consumed by our consumer culture that we tend to think of guitars as impossibly complex devices that somebody else has to build. One of the many beauties of the cigar box guitar is that it shatters this myth.

You see, while stringed instruments are bound by certain laws of physics, the golden rule of cigar box guitar building is that there are no rules. There's no right way, no master plan, no industry standard for the design. Each instrument is its own unique answer to the question: What is a cigar box guitar?

Let's take a look at the physical heart of the matter for another possible answer.

It's likely it all started with a taut cord.

Perhaps, as some writers have suggested, that cord was part of an archer's bow. Some musically attuned hunter or warrior must have liked the sound made by that vibrating bowstring when it caused the air around it to vibrate. He may have noticed how the pitch changed with the tension of the string.

I imagine some off-duty archer noodling out a tune on his bow string while bracing one end of the bow against a log or a board. The vibrations transferred to the wood produced a louder sound.

Now imagine that the bow was braced against a hollow log. Suddenly the sound was quite a bit louder, amplified and focused by the vibrations of the air inside the hollow log.

From a physical standpoint, that's really all there is to a cigar box guitar: a taut, vibrating cord (usually a steel guitar string); a vibrating wooden surface over a hollow, resonating chamber (usually a wooden cigar box); and a point of contact between the string and the wood (called the bridge).

Let's leave our imaginary archer now and fast-forward to the United States of America, late in the nineteenth century.

In many parts of the country, people didn't have much. The idea of dropping $3,700 at Guitar Works on a Collings or a Taylor belonged to the distant, unimaginable future.

But people still made music. It's like they needed to make music, and we humans are a resourceful lot.

In a world without manufactured guitars, a person could hammer two nails into a board and stretch a strand of wire pulled from a screen door tightly

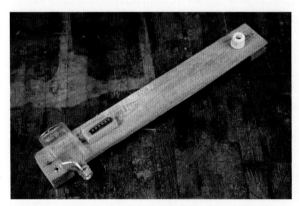

This simple yet playable modern-day diddley bow by an unknown builder is made from barn wood, a whiskey bottle, and a ceramic insulator.

between the nails. Ramming a block of wood under one end would give the wire still more tension.

Plucking that wire or striking it with a stick would cause the wire to vibrate. As the wire vibrated, it would cause the air around it to vibrate, and a sweet, simple tone would resonate. Moving an empty bottle or a piece of pipe along the string while plucking would change the length of the vibrating section of wire. That, in turn, would change the wavelength of the airborne vibrations, which would vary the pitch of that tone. Adding in a little rhythm would be enough to get people singing and dancing.

Ethnomusicologists define this primitive, one-stringed instrument as a monochord zither. Colloquially, it's more often called a diddley bow.

The diddley bow's drawback is its limited volume. The volume can be pumped up a bit by wedging a jar or can under the string to act as a resonating chamber, but that, too, has limits. Fortunately for our mid-nineteenth century musicians, help was on the way.

While the details of its history may be a bit sketchy—objects this humble don't get much play in the history books—we have enough information to speculate about the cigar box guitar's origins.

In the early nineteenth century, cigars were shipped in barrels or bundled in smaller quantities in pig bladders. The mid-nineteenth century saw the introduction of the cedar cigar box, tailor-made to hold twenty-five cigars in three rows—eight in the bottom row, nine in the middle row, and eight again on top.

In order to help fund the Civil War, President Lincoln's congress began taxing a broad range of consumer goods, including cigars. Tax stamps were issued for fixed quantities of cigars and the cedar 8/9/8 box, sealed with a U.S. tax stamp, rapidly became, and remains, the industry standard for packaging cigars.

An etching titled *Home, sweet home* by Edwin Forbes, circa 1876, shows a winter camp scene during the Civil War and is cited as the earliest documentation of cigar box instruments.

Cedar keeps cigars fresh. As luck would have it, cedar also makes an excellent tone wood. In fact, it's sometimes used in fine guitar building. It didn't take long before someone figured out that those little boxes, emptied of cigars, made ideal resonating chambers to amplify vibrating strings. Cigar boxes were soon pressed into service by resourceful instrument builders.

With the addition of a string or two, and sometimes a horsehair bow, builders could have a playable guitar or fiddle. Indeed, the earliest definitive reference we have of a cigar box instrument is a print of a Civil War soldier drawing a bow across a cigar box fiddle.

Americans built and played cigar box guitars and fiddles throughout the first half of the twentieth century. They remained common right up through World War II. In fact, in some of earlier Peanuts comic strips from the '50s, Charlie Brown played a cigar box guitar. Throughout this book are Vintage Spotlights on preserved antique builds from decades—even centuries—ago. Because of the cigar box guitar's humble origins, most builders of these instruments remain unknown.

Despite their popularity, however, as we moved toward the '60s, the guitars all but disappeared from the scene.

What happened to cigar box guitars?

After World War II, American culture took a dramatic shift toward consumerism and, specifically, the mass consumption of manufactured goods. We entered an era where Americans began looking down their noses at the humble and the homemade. Guitars became something people bought from Sears or Montgomery Ward.

But if cigar box guitars had disappeared altogether, you would not be holding this book. Something stimulated a twenty-first century revival of this nearly extinct bit of populist culture. What happened?

Moses Williams plays the diddley bow for a group of boys in Waverly, Florida, sometime before 1982.

This might be a good time to talk about my own introduction to cigar box guitars and to look at how I became the chief propaganda minister of this musical revolution.

In 2006, when she was about five years old, my daughter began taking an interest in my guitars. I wanted her to have a guitar of her own. My father had told me about cigar box guitars when I was a kid, but I didn't have much more to go on other than this vague concept. I began poking around the Internet to see if I could find some ideas.

My search engines turned up perhaps two modest references to cigar box guitars. I had imagined something made from a cardboard box and rubber bands, but instead I found instructions for building playable guitars capable of making real music.

Using wooden cigar boxes, pieces of 1" x 2" (2 x 4cm) maple salvaged from a neighbor's rehab project, used guitar tuners, bolts, guitar strings, and some glue, I built my daughter and myself a pair of three-string guitars. They made a surprisingly pleasing sound, and building them was a lot of fun.

I built another cigar box guitar after that, and then another, trying slightly different approaches with each build to solve problems I'd encountered in the construction of my previous builds. After five guitars, I set building aside for a while.

Several years later, browsing through a book called *The Little Book of Whittling*, I noticed a brief message on the copyright page: something like, if you have an idea for a woodworking book, we want to hear about it.

I sent Fox Chapel Publishing an email with pictures of the guitars I'd built, along with some samples of my writing. My timing was fortuitous. Several conversations later, my idea for a modest how-to pamphlet had grown into a concept for a hundred-page book that would contain not only

My obsession with cigar box guitars began as I built two: one for me and one for my daughter.

13

three illustrated how-to-build sections, but also a photo gallery of cigar box instruments and profiles of people who build and play cigar box guitars.

I soon discovered that a lot of other people had become curious about cigar box guitars during the years since I had first looked into the subject. By 2010, a huge, vibrant, international cigar box guitar community had blossomed. Thousands of builders were now busy not just building guitars, but also interacting across websites, blogs, social networking sites, eBay, YouTube, and at festivals around the country.

The materials I gathered for our hundred-page book about this humble, homemade musical instrument ultimately filled more than two hundred pages—and now a second book!

What happened to create this explosion of interest in a primitive musical instrument that had been on the brink of extinction? Call it synchronicity—a confluence of characters and conditions.

It does not surprise me that this sudden explosion of interest in homemade fun coincided with the implosion of the U.S. economy in 2008. Perhaps a lot of people who had been buying or thinking about buying expensive, boutique-built guitars suddenly found themselves without the resources to do so. Their priorities shifted. With so many Americans in the same financial boat, the idea of banging on something humble and homemade became less shameful. It took on a different air.

A huge population of dream-deferring baby boomers, who'd grown up knowing they were born to rock, found themselves with empty nests, a little bit of time on their hands, and fifty- to sixty-year-old faces looking back at them from their bathroom mirrors saying, "Now or never." This latent revolution just needed a catalyst, and it soon got one.

Just a few years before the economic downturn, a man named Shane Speal had embraced the cigar box guitar with a truly religious fervor. Speal began laying the groundwork for a musical revolution with missionary zeal.

From the age of eight, Speal had played guitar. When he finished high school, he decided that he wanted to be a minister, so he enrolled in a bible college in Lancaster, Pennsylvania. He says he was "big into Christian rock" at the time, but soon found that style of music a little "too plastic" for his taste.

After a year, he transferred to Indiana University of Pennsylvania, and it was there that he discovered

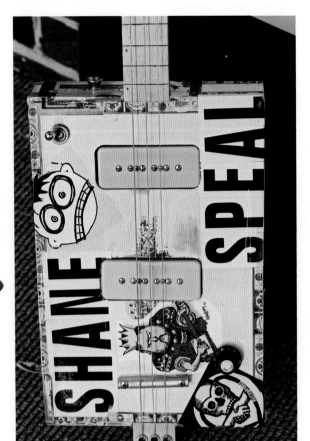

Tomi-O Hartwell built this three-string cigar box guitar as a tribute to Shane Speal, King of the Cigar Box Guitar. (From the collection of Shane Speal.)

the blues. Speal says after discovering Jimi Hendrix and Jimmy Paige, he wanted to know who had influenced them. "You take one step back and you get Muddy Waters and Hound Dog Taylor. Who influenced them? You take one step back and you get Robert Johnson and Blind Willy Johnson." Nothing if not thorough, Speal then wanted to know who had influenced those guys—the very earliest blues men. What was that "one step deeper than the delta blues"? He couldn't find any leads. Their predecessors predated recorded music.

Then Shane Speal discovered the cigar box guitar. I spoke with Speal in 2010 about his discovery and about his unusual passion for this humble instrument:

———————⟨◇⟩———————

SPEAL: *A friend of mine gave me a bunch of his dad's old* Guitar Player *magazines. There was an article from 1976. It was how to build [a cigar box guitar] based on a Carl Perkins interview with* Guitar Player. *Carl Perkins started out on a two-string cigar box guitar. Some guy made a really crude version of it and published it in* Guitar Player *magazine. I went nuts.*

SUTTON: *A minute ago you said you had thought you wanted to be a preacher. Now you're preaching the cigar box guitar gospel. How did that come about?*

SPEAL: *I am. I know it sounds absurd for me to say, but I was at one point at a very low point in my life, and I was just praying my guts out, and honest—I am not [kidding] at all—I was praying and I felt, show the world the cigar box guitar. This was in 2002 or 2003. That's what I felt my calling was. Why? It made no sense to me. I had been playing other homemade instruments. I made a Dobro out of a mailbox and a few other things, but I just felt this calling: "Show the world the cigar box guitar."*

———————⟨◇⟩———————

IMAGES OF INGENUITY

Modern day builders find inspiration in all sorts of places when crafting their unique cigar box guitars. Here are just a few examples.

This guitar by Paul "Uncle Pauly" Bessette uses a rusty old can lid as a resonator, an iron retaining ring as a biscuit, a rusted bolt as a bridge, and a spoon as an ornamental string anchor.

Music will be made. This "canjo," built by Glenn Kaiser, uses a tin bean can as a resonating chamber.

Builder Al Hamilton of Snow Shoe, Pennsylvania made one guitar so that it could be opened up and used to carry items—such as makeup, shown here.

Lloyd "MadMan" Madansky of Arroyo Grande, California, built this crutch six-string cigar box guitar. (From the collection of Shane Speal.)

15

Violin maker Peter Seman acquired this antique cigar box violin and restored it in his Skokie, Illinois violin shop. The original maker is unknown. The piece is a true testament to the deep connection between the past and present of cigar box guitars.

Shane Speal crowned himself the "self-proclaimed king of the cigar box guitar" and began his ministry on the Internet. He built a one-page website on Geocities explaining, in simple terms, how to build a cigar box guitar. He put the plans up for free.

His timing could not have been more perfect. Just a few years later, the economy tanked and a lot of those born-to-rock baby boomers were no longer able to buy hand-built Martins and Taylors to enjoy in their retirement. Time was running short on getting their blues/rock grooves on. They began to improvise.

Propelled by this groundswell of interest in homemade instruments, and in cigar box guitars in particular, Speal's Geocities page quickly evolved into a Yahoo group that then evolved into a social-networking site called Cigar Box Nation.

By April 2013, Cigar Box Nation boasted 10,000 members from all around the world. In ten short years, Speal's ministry, which started with a website and "a couple of pieces of shop equipment between the washer and dryer," had reached the stars. Rock legend Sir Paul McCartney played a cigar box guitar with members of Nirvana at a benefit concert in December of 2012, and again later that week on *Saturday Night Live.*

So, what is a cigar box guitar? With any community of this size, you'll have more than a few opinions on the subject. Some will argue that if it has frets, it's not a cigar box guitar, while others rail against amplification. Still others may speak with disdain about the six-string, solid-body in a cigar box wrapper.

Generally, though, cigar box guitar people are a friendly bunch who'll help you find your own answers. And when you start asking questions, you'll soon become addicted, too. Whether you decide to build, collect, or just admire these slices of history and ingenuity, you'll soon be just as addicted as the rest of us. Our obsession will become yours—and that's a good thing.

With that, I'd like to extend my thanks to this busy, diverse community for extending themselves to me and making it possible for me to assemble this collection of photos. Some of these photos were taken while I was making *Cigar Box Guitars,* and many others have been taken in the years since that book was released.

In photographing the guitars for these books, I have tried to make photos that are as informative as they are attractive. I hope that these photos inspire you, if you haven't already taken the plunge, to grab a box and join the revolution.

—DAVID SUTTON

BUILD / PLAY / REPEAT!

THE GUITARS

RIGHT
This Red Dog Guitars three-string electric
was built by John McNair of Puerto Rico.
(From the collection of Shane Speal.)

BELOW
John used a double-coil pickup set at
an angle to amplify this three-string build.

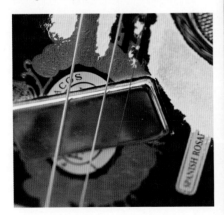

ABOVE
Josh added boost and frequency expansion switches and a volume control knob.

LEFT
This Smokehouse Cohiba six-string electric was built by Josh Gayou of Smokehouse Guitars in Southern California. Josh uses three paired sets of strings. (From the collection of Shane Speal.)

<o>

CARL PERKINS

"Before I went to school, I started fooling around on guitar. My daddy made me one with a cigar box, a broomstick, and two strands of baling wire and I'd sit and beat on that thing."

ABOVE
This ingenious instrument is a
thumb piano. Designed by art teacher
Diane Sutliff of Chicago, it combines
a compact cigar box, an oak dowel,
brass wire, and screws.

RIGHT
A detail of Diane's thumb piano shows
the fixtures at the tail end.

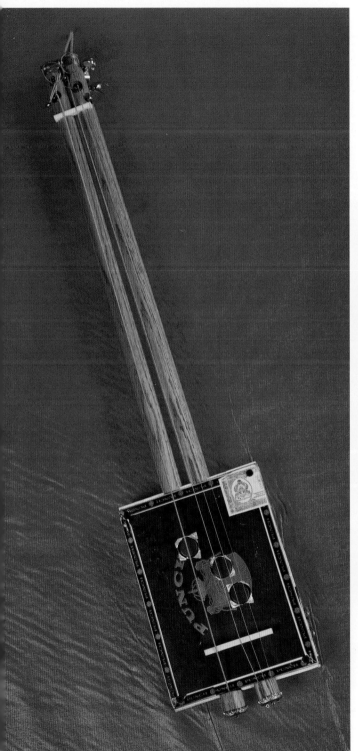

LEFT
This double-neck cigar box bass/guitar was built by John Lowe of Xanadu Music in Memphis, Tennessee, and is owned by Bill Jehle, frontman of the Alabama-based band Nadaband.

BELOW
Take a close look at the tuners and nut on this four-string *Lowebow*. A single piece of composite spans both necks, providing a string nut for both guitar and bass sides.

23

ABOVE
A detail shows the tail end and string anchors on the double-neck *Lowebow*. John uses bottle caps to keep the strings from tearing into the wood.

RIGHT
This three-string cigar box guitar by Polk County, Florida builder Travis "Uncle Crow" Richardson uses board-on-box construction, as opposed to "stick through" construction, and eyebolts with wing nuts as friction tuners. This guitar resides in the lobby of the Holiday Music Motel in Sturgeon Bay, Wisconsin.

BELOW
Travis used eyebolts, nuts, wingnuts, and washers to create tuners for this board-on-box guitar.

ABOVE
An angled cutoff provides an elegantly simple string-anchoring solution.

LEFT
No cigar box is immune to guitar building! Different builders have different favorites, but the Revolucion cigar box used by this unknown builder shows that you can use the box you have. You can also get a surprising range of music from just two strings. This guitar also uses diatonic fretting. Note that a door strike plate has been implemented to anchor the strings. (From the collection of Bill Jehle.)

ABOVE
This two-stringer features a small threaded bolt as a string nut and screw-eyes for string trees.

RIGHT
I built this three-string acoustic cigar box guitar for Build #1 in my first book, *Cigar Box Guitars*.

ABOVE
A detail shot shows the headstock for Build #1.

RIGHT
I used a J-bolt to provide the string bridge for Build #1.

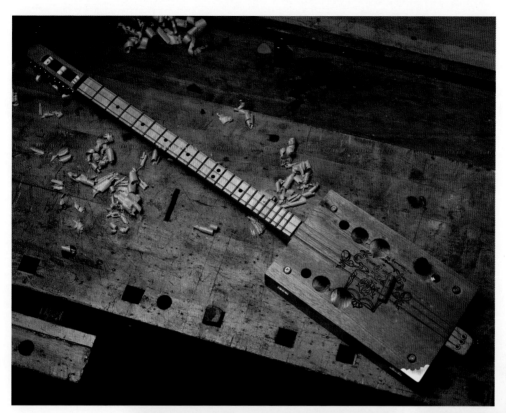

LEFT
Build #2 adds frets
and a piezo pickup
into the mix.

ABOVE
I added a carved cherry volume
knob to Build #2.

LEFT
A detail shows the body for Build #2.

BELOW
A nicely built Fonseca one-string guitar was fashioned
from a broom handle and a cigar box by an unknown
maker. (From the collection of Bill Jehle.)

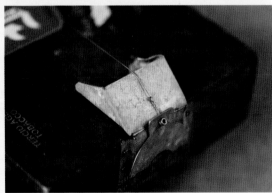

ABOVE
The bent scrap-metal that serves as
a bridge and saddle gives this guitar
a very bright, powerful, and clear tone.

LEFT
The guitar tuner used on this one-string
is held in place with a bent nail.

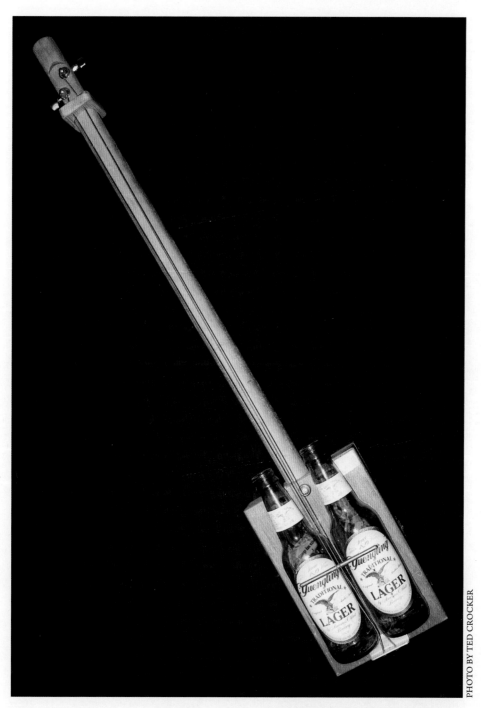

For this experimental two-string guitar,
builder and Handmade Music Clubhouse host
(*handmademusicclubhouse.com*) Ted Crocker
used empty beer bottles as resonators and
an oak dowel for a neck.

TOP
A detail shows the mother-of-pearl inlay work in John's fingerboard.

BOTTOM
This electric four-string was built by John Terrell of Huntsville, Alabama.

ABOVE
Rick Springfield's fan club commissioned luthier Matty Baratto of North Hollywood, California, to build this four-string acoustic as a gift for the singer. Matty also built the four-string guitar Paul McCartney famously played with members of Nirvana at the Hurricane Sandy benefit concert and later on *Saturday Night Live*. (From the collection of Bill Jehle.)

LEFT
Matty overlaid the headstock with birdseye maple and carved the nut out of ebony.

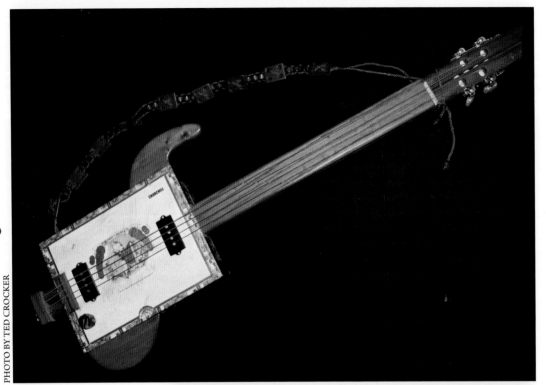

ABOVE
Ted Crocker built the neck for this four-string electric guitar using paired oak dowels with a board attached to the front as a fretless fretboard. Two four-pole magnetic pickups provide the drive.

RIGHT
He attached carved wood details to the box to enhance its appearance and increase the player's comfort.

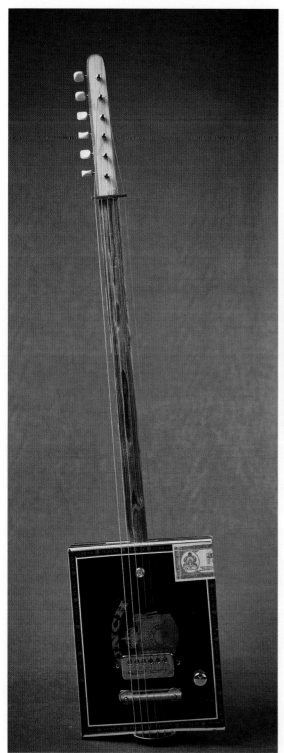

LEFT
Huntsville, Alabama, cigar box guitar builder and collector Bill Jehle challenged himself to build a guitar out of scraps he had lying around. The result: this six-string fretless guitar built for less than $2 (he says he paid a dollar for the pickup).

BELOW
Bill fashioned a bridge for his junk guitar out of a comb he found at a gas station.

33

JIMI HENDRIX

"Eight-year-old James Marshall Hendrix wanted so much to play the guitar to set his poems to music that he used a broom to strum out the rhythms in his head until he crafted a cigar box into his own guitar." Jimi's cigar box guitar had rubber bands wrapped around the box, serving as strings.

34

TOP
"Exotic Coconut, Exhilarating Rum, Exciting Taste." How could this Nukii cookie tin guitar by Diane Sutliff not inspire a party?

BOTTOM
Pop-rivet collars reinforce the string anchor holes and keep the strings from biting into the wood.

LEFT
A close-up photograph of the headstock shows *The Chugger's* tuners.

BELOW
Shane Speal calls this ultra simple two-string build *The Chugger*. Look for Shane and his Chugger on YouTube for an amazing demonstration of what kind of music can be drawn out of just two strings.

36

TOP

In the hands of pat mAcdonald the instrument that gave his band a name takes on a life of its own.

BOTTOM

This view shows the dual outputs in action. Having one output for the bass and one for the guitar strings allows the two signals to be processed differently.

RIGHT

This double-necked bass/guitar hybrid developed by Memphis, Tennessee, instrument builder John Lowe does most of the heavy lifting for the band Purgatory Hill. Lowe dubbed this instrument the Purgatory Hill Harp—and the instrument then lent the band its name.

RIGHT
John favors bottle caps to serve as string anchors on his *Lowebow* creations.

BELOW
John's autograph and inscription appear on the back of pat mAcdonald's *Purgatory Hill Harp*.

LEFT
Builder John Lowe ingeniously perches two magnetic pickups in a shared arrangement under the three guitar strings. A third pickup for the bass string is visible at the top edge of the frame. John uses sewing machine bobbins, ultra fine copper wire, and tiny magnets to tailor his pickups for his signature sound.

ABOVE
pat mAcdonald plays in York, Pennsylvania, 2010.

BELOW
pat performs with his Purgatory Hill Harp in Chicago, 2012.

LEFT
pat mAcdonald and melaniejane rest up in York, Pennsylvania after headlining the 2010 Cigar Box Guitar Festival.

ABOVE
pat mAcdonald does double duty on stage in York, Pennsylvania, 2010.

LEFT
pat wears his slide on his pinkie finger.

RIGHT
Shane Speal built this three-string in 1996 and has used it continuously since, giving it the nickname "Old Faithful."

BELOW
A detail shot shows *Old Faithful's* headstock.

ABOVE
Shane collects autographs from musicians he's shared the stage with. Many of them surround the sound hole on this three-string.

VINTAGE SPOTLIGHT

RIGHT
Though he acquired these two one-string guitars from different sources, Bill Jehle calls them "sisters," because they appear to be built by the same unknown maker. Discovered at two separate auctions, they date to the 1930s and came from upstate New York. Each has a single, mechanical guitar tuner and otherwise all-wood construction.

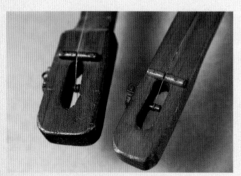

ABOVE
Slotted headstocks are equipped with geared, mechanical tuning machines.

TOP
Paul Bessette of Uncle Pauly's Boxes in Cockeysville, Maryland fashioned this three-string resonator from a rusted can lid, and then used an iron retaining ring as a biscuit and a rusted bolt for a bridge. He used stained oak for a fretboard over a red oak neck. A spoon serves as an ornamental string anchor and tailpiece.

BOTTOM
A close-up photo shows the resonator/biscuit/bridge assembly.

42

This La Floridana four-string acoustic/electric by an unknown builder has volume and tone controls for a piezo pickup and uses large grommets to adorn the sound holes. (From the collection of Bill Jehle.)

LIGHTNIN HOPKINS

"So I went ahead and made me a guitar. I got me a cigar box, I cut me a round hole in the middle of it, take me a little piece of plank, nailed it onto that cigar box, and I got me some screen wire and I made me a bridge back there and raised it up high enough that it would sound inside that little box, and got me a tune out of it. I kept my tune and I played from then on."

BELOW
Al's guitar has Indian head pennies embedded in the neck and tailstock.

ABOVE
Al Hamilton of Snow Shoe, Pennsylvania, built this three-string York Imperial acoustic. (From the collection of Shane Speal.)

LEFT
An Indian head nickel inlay adorns the neck.

VINTAGE SPOTLIGHT

RIGHT
This single-string cigar box guitar or fiddle
was built around the turn of the last century.
Its maker is unknown. (From the collection
of Shane Speal.)

ABOVE
A headstock detail shows
the hand-whittled tuning peg.

Michael Ballerini of Clawson, Michigan built this acoustic soprano ukulele around an antique cigar box, using a set neck as opposed to a through neck. He used old-growth cherry for both the neck and the fretboard.

LEFT
Michael gave this ukulele a set neck
as opposed to a stick-through box neck.

BELOW
Shoe Peg was a brand of cigar sold by
the Erlinda Cigar Company of Wisconsin.

RIGHT
This fretless resonator guitar appeared during the 2010 CBG Extravaganza in Huntsville, Alabama. The builder is unknown. (From the collection of Bill Jehle.)

BELOW
The builder used a found metal object as a resonator. This photo also shows a wooden biscuit between the bridge and the resonator.

BELOW
Tomi-O Hartwell's guitar was designed as a
six-string version of Shane Speal's "Old Faithful."
(From the collection of Shane Speal.)

TOP
Tomi-O used three sets of paired strings
on this build for a fuller sound.

MIDDLE
Shane Speal's autograph adorns this
Tomi-O custom build.

BOTTOM
Screws and washers are used as string
trees in Tomi-O's six-string version of
Shane Speal's "Old Faithful."

RIGHT
Al Hamilton built this guitar as a gift
for Purgatory Hill's melaniejane.

TOP
An antique box and an old wrench make up most
of this guitar. Wait...Did someone say makeup?

BOTTOM
Al built this cigar box guitar so that it could
be opened to reveal a makeup mirror and
other girlie essentials.

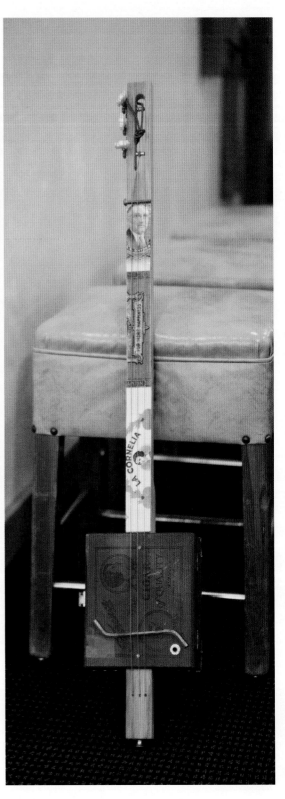

LEFT
This super-simple two-string instrument resulted from my attempt to use a minimal number of very simple tools and materials to make a playable instrument. I used the handle from a broken lawn implement, a drill, sandpaper, and a couple of screws.

BELOW
I attached a piece of adhesive sandpaper to the neck dowel and used that to shape both the nut and the bridge of this guitar.

LEFT
Built by Tomi-O Hartwell, this Padron double-neck electric body cigar box guitar has two switched single-coil guitar pickups. (From the collection of Shane Speal.)

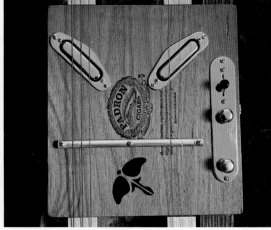

ABOVE
The guitar splits a standard set of guitar strings—bass strings on top and lighter strings on the bottom.

RIGHT
Daddy Mojo is a full-time cigar box guitar building enterprise started in Montreal by artist and builder Lenny Piroth-Robert. His acoustic three-string on the right has an oak neck and uses a bolt as a nut. Both guitars use picture-hanging hardware for string trees. The five-string on the left is more recent and has a piezo pickup, a maple neck, and a plastic nut. It's also built around a custom-order cedar box, while the older instrument uses a repurposed box. (From the collection of Bill Jehle.)

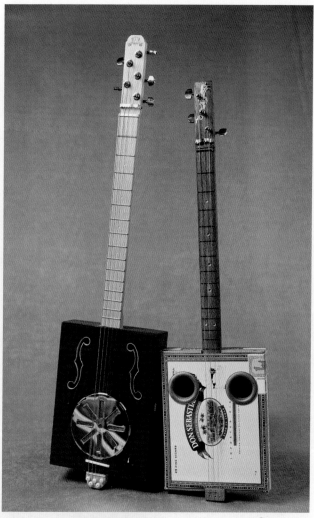

53

ABOVE LEFT
The five-string has an older Daddy Mojo logo on the headstock and a newer one on the back of the box.

ABOVE RIGHT
In the early years, Lenny decorated his headstocks with cigar labels, as shown on the headstock of the three-string guitar.

LEFT
The three-string bears the original Daddy Mojo logo, a frog playing a banjo, in the center of the back.

PHOTO BY MIKE LOWE

Mike Lowe (aka Old Lowe) of Rockwall, Texas built this four-string acoustic guitar/dulcimer hybrid with diatonic fretting from a Padron box (favored by many builders for its tone and beautiful grain patterns). He used red oak for the neck. The highest string (called the melody string by dulcimer players) is doubled so the two strings are played as one for a fuller sound. He adorned the corners with stencil work and the sound hole with a pull-tab.

LEFT
This John Lowe creation belongs to singer/songwriter/multi-instrumentalist melaniejane, who performs with singer/songwriter pat mAcdonald as the cigar box guitar–based duo Purgatory Hill.

BELOW
This view of melaniejane's *Lowebow Lyre* shows the dual output system (one for the bass string and one for the guitar strings) and builder John Lowe's signature bottle cap string anchors.

GEORGE BENSON

The eight-time Grammy winner started his career as "Little Georgie Benson, the Kid From Gilmore Alley," playing a cigar box ukulele on street corners.

Diane Sutliff used the lid from a retired paint can to create a resonator for this little (17" [43cm] scale) three-string guitar.

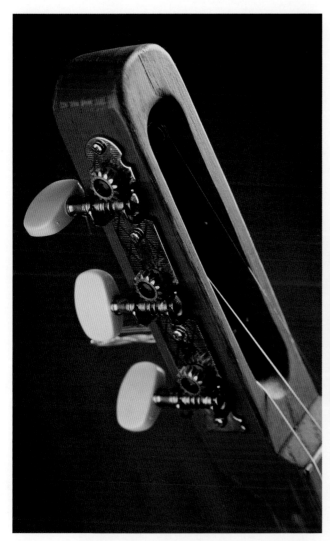

LEFT
Diane built the neck/headstock profile by gluing three pieces of pre-shaped oak molding together. As you can see, this profile provides ample "string break" to keep the strings secure against the nut.

RIGHT
A simple hinge makes a perfect tailpiece for this build.

Microwave Dave Gallaher,
Huntsville, Alabama, 2010.

TOP
Microwave Dave Gallaher plays
on stage at the Cigar Box Guitar
Extravaganza in Huntsville,
Alabama, 2010.

BOTTOM
John Lowe, aka Johnny Lowebow,
at the Holiday Music Festival in
Sturgeon Bay, Wisconsin.

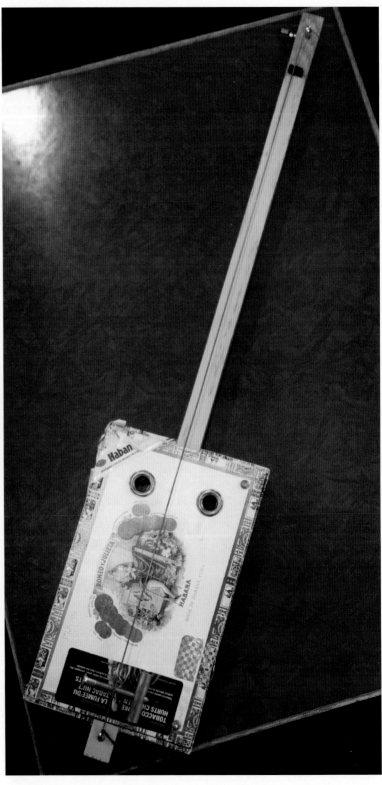

ABOVE
Uncle Crow used a furniture fastener as
a bridge on his one-string cigar box guitar.

RIGHT
This super-simple, single-string guitar was
constructed by Travis "Uncle Crow" Richardson.
It resides in the lobby of the Holiday Music Motel
in Sturgeon Bay, Wisconsin.

PHOTO BY MIKE LOWE

This ingenious banjo/guitar/ dulcimer hybrid is by Mike Lowe. Mike started with a Padron box to build a five-string. The fifth string begins at the fifth fret like a five-string banjo, but the tuner for the fifth string is located at the tail end of the instrument. Mike used diatonic (dulcimer) fretting and a short 15" scale. He fashioned the bridge from bois d'earc (also called osage orange).

ABOVE
Darren fashioned a decorative bridge out of scraps for his three-string.

RIGHT
This custom order was made by Darren Brown of Nova Scotia for Shane Speal. (From the collection of Shane Speal.)

LEFT
This colorful three-string Deco guitar by Chicago builder Jeremiah Lee is reminiscent of a dramatic sunset.

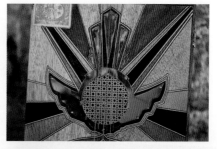

TOP
Jeremiah's intricate application of stains and dyes, embellished with metalwork, creates dramatic visuals.

MIDDLE
Jeremiah puts a great deal of thought into pieces like this rosewood saddle. Note how the shape echoes the decorative coloring.

BOTTOM
Jeremiah used an unusual configuration to fit three tuners into this head stock.

VINTAGE SPOTLIGHT

RIGHT
Both of these antique pieces date from the late nineteenth century. Their makers are unknown. (From the collection of Bill Jehle.)

BELOW
One of the oldest instruments in Bill Jehle's collection, this violin is initialed and dated by the builder: A. H. B. '89 (as in 1889). In 1994, Shane Speal commissioned luthiers Jeff Hostetter and Amy Hopkins to restore the violin to a fully playable condition. Two years and many shop hours later, it was returned to Speal, strung up, and ready for the concert stage.

RIGHT
This cigar box ukulele was purchased by Bill Jehle at an estate auction. The accompanying note indicates it was built around 1892 as a gift for an uncle named Albert Leiff.

AN OBSESSION WITH CIGAR BOX GUITARS

ABOVE
The tuners are arranged three on each vertical member.

LEFT
Lloyd "Madman" Madansky of Arroyo Grande, California, built this crutch six-string cigar box guitar. (From the collection of Shane Speal.)

VINTAGE SPOTLIGHT

ABOVE
A detail of the headstock shows the hand-carved nut and tuners.

RIGHT
This tiny ukulele was built from the wood of a discarded cigar box by an unknown maker. Collector Bill Jehle calls it "inside out" because the wood was reversed so that the box's label is visible on the inside of the ukulele. Though it's more a piece of folk art than a playable instrument, the one remaining string testifies that it once made music.

LEFT
The first *Purgatory Hill Harp* had the two oak dowels set far apart (see page 115). Blues musician Richard Johnston eventually convinced builder John Lowe to bring the two necks closer together so he could use a conventional slide to play the instrument.

BELOW
For this *Purgatory Hill Harp*, John added a sculpted wooden armrest.

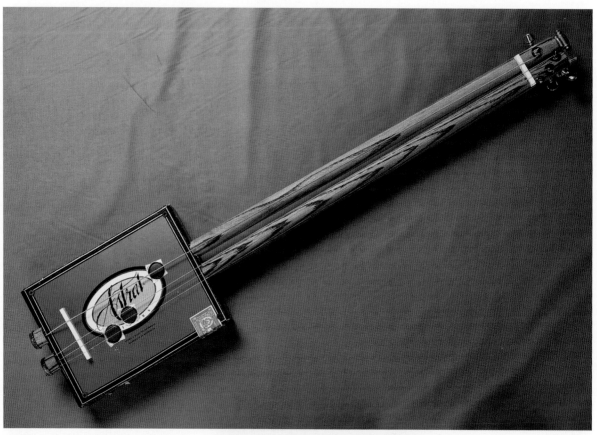

ABOVE
Builder John Lowe ingeniously perches two magnetic pickups in a shared arrangement under the three guitar strings in this bass/ guitar hybrid.

RIGHT
A close-up shows the tuner configuration.

LEFT
Lenny Piroth-Robert photographed this four-string *Tenor Clydesdale* model with a mini-humbucker pickup at the Daddy Mojo factory in Montreal.

BELOW
Natural finish and twin f-holes give the *Clydesdale* an understated elegance.

PHOTO COURTESY DADDY MOJO GUITARS

PHOTO COURTESY DADDY MOJO GUITARS

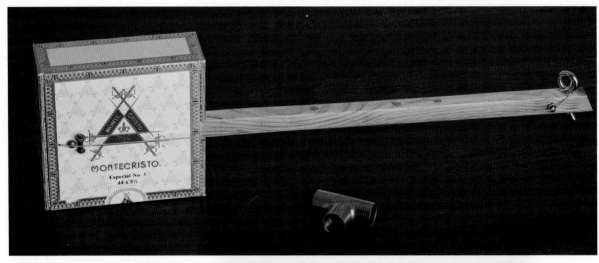

ABOVE
Built and played by Chicago's Glenn Kaiser
(whose Resurrection Band, 1972–2000,
revolutionized Christian music), this single-
string instrument employs a simple pine neck,
thumbtacks for position markers, an eyebolt
tuner, and a copper plumbing part for a slide.

RIGHT
Here's a close up of the eyebolt Glenn used
for a tuner. Note also the slotted brass screw
he uses as a string nut.

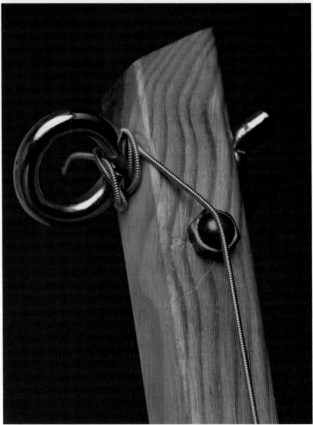

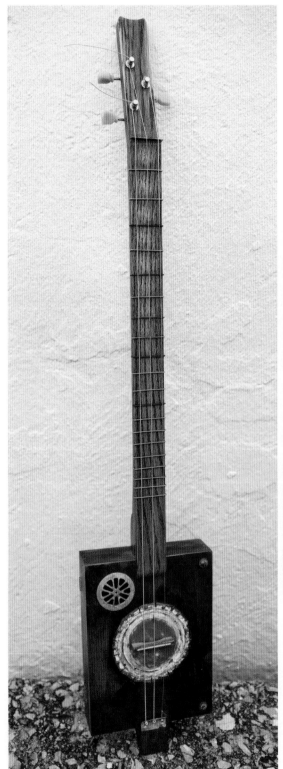

LEFT

Paul "Uncle Pauly" Bessette made frets for this three-string paint can lid resonator guitar by embedding copper wire into the oak neck. Red frets act as position markers.

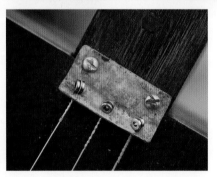

TOP

Paul used a piece of oak and a cut-off finish nail to make the saddle and bridge for this guitar.

BOTTOM

A piece of tarnished metal makes an artful string anchor.

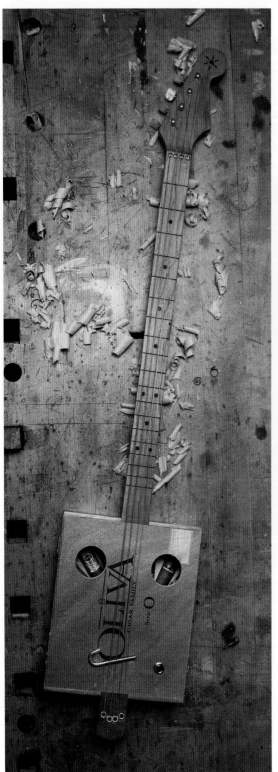

BELOW LEFT
When I built guitar #5, I decided I was going to get this headstock thing right! Fender inspired the shape, and I equipped it with a half-set of mandolin tuners.

BELOW RIGHT
I also experimented with using slotted screws as a nut. I had to file out the slots for the heavier strings. For the lighter strings, setting the slot at a slight angle prevented the string from buzzing in the slot.

ABOVE
Feeding a penchant for unexpected visuals, I turned to an issue of *Cigar Aficionado* for artwork to line this box.

LEFT
This Oliva four-string acoustic is also equipped with a piezo pickup. I used a thin hand saw to cut away the headstock area so it recedes from the fretboard. I created a nut by lining up four brass slotted screws and glued wood wings on the sides of the headstock area so I could cut it into an homage to a Fender Telecaster. I can't identify the wood I used for the neck other than to say that it was left over from a neighborhood remodeling job—and it's really pretty. Pecan has been suggested.

VINTAGE SPOTLIGHT

RIGHT
This fiddle was made from an Owl cigar box by an unknown builder. The bow was also hand carved. The name of the builder and the vintage of the build are both lost to time. (From the collection of Bill Jehle.)

ABOVE
A detail shows the owl carved into the headstock.

RIGHT
The maker of this fiddle carried the owl theme into the creation of the fiddle's sound holes.

RIGHT

I built these two three-string cigar box guitars side by side (one for me and one for my daughter) using salvaged tuners and some maple off-cuts from a neighbor's remodeling project. Both guitars are acoustic. The good news about these two cigar box guitars is that they sound great owing in part to the fortuitous choice of maple for the necks. I made the headstocks a bit too short—lesson learned.

BELOW

For one guitar, I made the nut out of a piece of oak dowel and used eye-screws for string trees.

LEFT

For the second guitar, I used a piece of natural horn set into a slot for the nut.

Texas builder Brian "Bairfoot Cajun" Romero crafted this Iron Mask three-string electric guitar. (From the collection of Shane Speal.)

RIGHT
Al Hamilton built this two-string around an antique King Oscar cigar box.

BELOW
Al used a salvaged saddle and bridge from an acoustic guitar on his three-string build.

---◆---

Roy Clark

The great country guitarist and banjo player (and Hee-Haw host) first played an instrument his father made from a cigar box and ukulele neck with four strings.

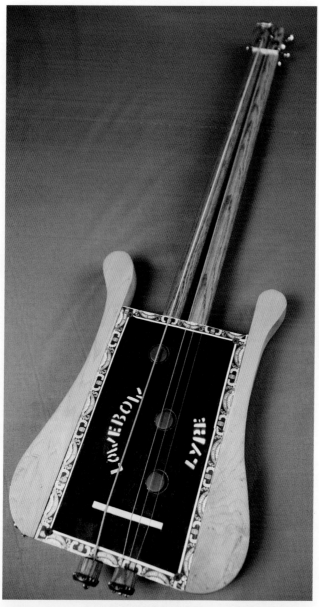

TOP
This *Lowebow Lyre* was fashioned
by builder John Lowe. (From the
collection of Bill Jehle.)

BOTTOM
John autographs and numbers
his creations.

Shane Speal, York,
Pennsylvania, 2010.

TOP
Shane Speal plays alongside his son Shane Jr. at the Cigar Box Guitar Festival in York, Pennsylvania, 2010.

BOTTOM
Justin Johnson, Chicago CBG Festival, 2012.

Violin maker Peter Seman collects unusual violins. He acquired this antique cigar box violin and restored it in his Skokie, Illinois, violin shop. The original maker is unknown.

LEFT
Peter added a new bridge and crafted a custom tailpiece and chin rest to restore this antique to playable condition.

BELOW
This antique box on Peter's restoration recalls a time when cigars sold two for a nickel.

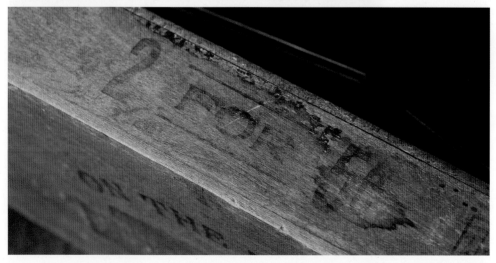

Huntsville, Alabama, builder John Nickel built
this board-on-box cigar box bass, which is
designed to mount on a microphone stand.
(From the collection of Bill Jehle.)

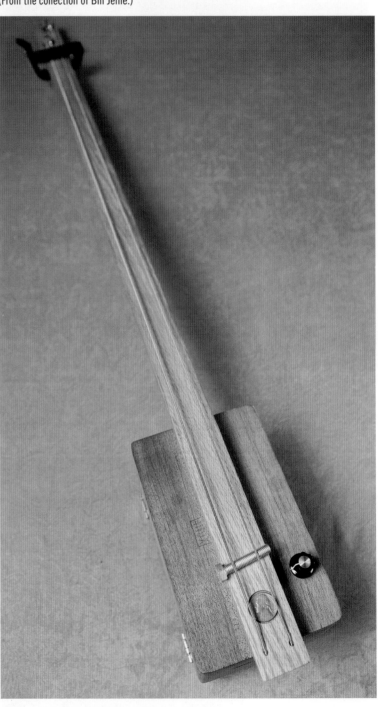

TOP
An interior shot of the bass shows a Radio Shack
piezo buzzer and mounting hardware.

BOTTOM
John included his signature inlay.

Tomi-O Hartwell built this three-string cigar box guitar as a tribute to Shane Speal, King of the Cigar Box Guitar. (From the collection of Shane Speal.)

BLUES LEGENDS ROBERT JOHNSON AND HIS STEPSON ROBERT LOCKWOOD JR.

"One day when Robert Johnson was taking a break from his roaming, he sat down to make a guitar with his young pupil Robert Lockwood Jr. What they made wasn't a diddley bow, the one-string instrument many fledgling bluesmen built by stretching a piece of wire between two nails. Johnson and Lockwood were intent on building something more sophisticated. Johnson shaped the wood and then made the body from a phonograph. Lockwood, who had been happily strumming away on Johnson's Stella, used the guitar for just over a year before it began to tear apart because 'we couldn't get the right type of glue.'"

RIGHT
Pennsylvania builder and author of *Handmade
Music Factory* Mike Orr repurposed an
old, enameled bedpan to create this unusual
fretless four-string electric guitar that he
named a "Shitar."

ABOVE
Mike left the label on as a tribute to the materials
and as a reminder to "relax."

BELOW
Mike floated a four-pole magnetic pickup beneath
the strings to enable amplified playing.

ABOVE
Detail of the giant brass fly. Let's say the extra weight improves this guitar's sustain.

LEFT
Steampunk Brundle Fly features Chicagoan Shawn Denman's own shop-built maple neck with an ebony-stained fretboard. This six-string electric has two individually switched single coil pickups and a hand-carved bone nut. Shawn used jumbo nickel/silver fret wire and crafted his own string trees out of brass. Yes, this guitar also sports a giant brass fly.

VINTAGE SPOTLIGHT

RIGHT
The unknown maker of this beautifully crafted antique four-string fiddle carved a deer's head into the headstock and also into the tip of the accompanying bow. The tailpiece and sound holes echo the deer motif. (From the collection of Bill Jehle.)

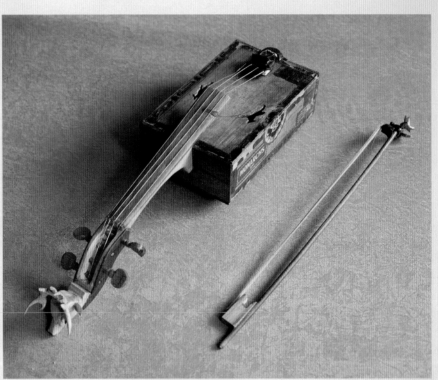

ABOVE
The tailpiece is held in place with braided twine. The fiddle has been outfitted with modern violin strings, but it's missing a bridge.

LEFT
A detailed view shows the deer carved into the headstock and bow.

PHOTO BY MIKE LOWE

PHOTO BY MIKE LOWE

ABOVE
Mike Lowe used red oak for the neck and overlaid a bois d'arc (osage orange) 16" (40.5cm) scale fretboard. He gave this guitar diatonic (dulcimer) fretting and doubled the melody string. The headstock has been adorned with an antique pull-tab.

LEFT
The bridge is built from red oak and bois d'arc.

RIGHT

This fretless three-string is the third cigar box guitar I built. I crafted it fairly early on, before there were online communities supporting builders with ideas and tips. For this build, I used a fancy Rocky Patel box with curved sides and a black lacquer finish. This build is my first to feature a piezo pickup. I used poplar for the neck, horn for the nut, and a scrap of rosewood for the bridge. The first time I plugged it in and strummed it, I was totally hooked.

ABOVE

I cut these sound holes with a hole saw. When I realized that the inside of the box could be seen through the larger sound holes, I opted to dress up the box's interior with a piece of Japanese art paper glued inside.

LEFT
Montreal builder Lenny Piroth-Robert, aka
Daddy Mojo, designed this four-string resonator
guitar using a custom-built box and handmade
resonator and cover.

BELOW
A detail shot shows the custom metalwork on
the Daddy Mojo *Resophonic*.

SLEEPY JOHN ESTES

Born January 25, 1904, in Ripley, TN, Sleepy John Estes
was one of a sharecropping family of ten. His father Daniel
was a guitarist, and this influenced his son to play.
Young Estes was blinded in his right eye from a baseball accident
at the age of six, limiting further athletic endeavors. His
interest in music prompted him to build crude guitars from cigar
boxes, which he played at local house parties as a child.

RIGHT
Steampunk Ophelia, a four-string acoustic/electric by Shawn Denman has a maple neck with a red-oak fretboard and jumbo nickel/silver frets with a bone nut. The fret dots are inlays of wire solder cut in cross-section. It uses a piezo pickup for amplification. Shawn inlaid a coin he found into the headstock. The sound hole cover is a repurposed computer fan guard. He used brass pipes to craft the arm rest and leg rest.

ABOVE
Shawn covered the tailpiece with brass and decorated it with earring parts. A skeleton key serves as the bridge.

VINTAGE SPOTLIGHT

RIGHT
The builder of this one-string fiddle is unknown, but the instrument comes from England. Still playable, it does not include the original bow. The case is hand built as well and bears a date stamp in the bottom inside that clearly reads, "December 24, 1920," suggesting this one-string fiddle was a Christmas gift.

BELOW
The builder carved this headstock right out of the neck.

RIGHT
The body of this one-string fiddle from the collection of Bill Jehle has elegant, book-matched f-holes.

RIGHT

My acoustic CAO Bat Wing three-string has a short (17" [43cm]) scale and diatonic fretting. The neck is from 100-year-old mahogany pulled out of the trash at a remodeling site. Following Diane Sutliff's lead, I used a scarf joint for the headstock and a zero fret as the nut. The fretboard is birdseye maple.

BELOW

In order to widen the headstock a bit, I glued another strip of mahogany to the side (Diane Sutliff calls these "wings") to provide support for the last tuner and to give me something to shape.

RIGHT

The tailpiece here is a small piece of carved ebony attached with two brass screws. I set a piece of fret wire into the ebony to keep the strings from cutting into the wood.

LEFT
On the bottom end, a hose clamp serves as a bridge. A ¼" (0.5cm) phono output jack is housed inside a copper coupling.

BELOW
The *Electric Lowebow Stick* by John Lowe is a remarkably fun and versatile instrument to play. It can be held like a guitar and thumb-strummed while the player presses the string against the dowel, or laid across a lap and played with a slide in the non-strumming hand.

93

ABOVE
Instead of a cigar box as a resonating chamber, the stick relies on a hand-wound, single-pole pickup plugged into the amplifier of your choice to bring up the volume.

LEFT
The stick's single string is tensioned and tuned with a guitar tuner. A screw serves as a nut.

BELOW
Created by builder John Lowe, the *Lowebow* (a bass/guitar hybrid)
appears in many iterations and seems to constantly evolve. This
Masonite one features a double resonator and a movable nut.
(From the collection of Bill Jehle.)

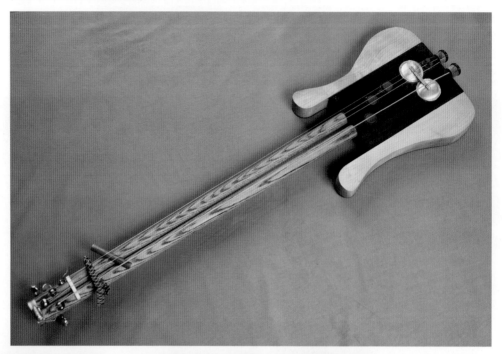

ABOVE
John's trademark bottle-cap string anchors adorn
the bottom of the guitar.

LEFT
John fits three tuners in a single dowel by spiraling
them around. The piece of titanium protruding from
beneath the strings is a movable nut, which he slides
up or down to instantly change keys, even in mid-song.

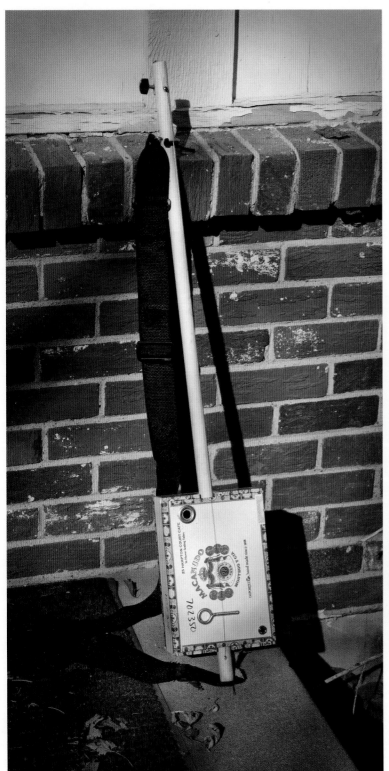

LEFT
Musician and cigar box guitar builder Kevin Kraft
has four children, and all have built and played
cigar box guitars. Kevin guided one of his children
in building this single-stringed instrument. What
a great way to spend family time together.

BELOW
The fretless guitar is the essence of simplicity.

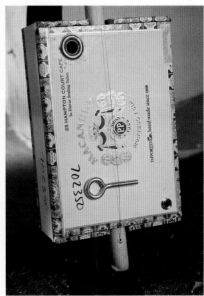

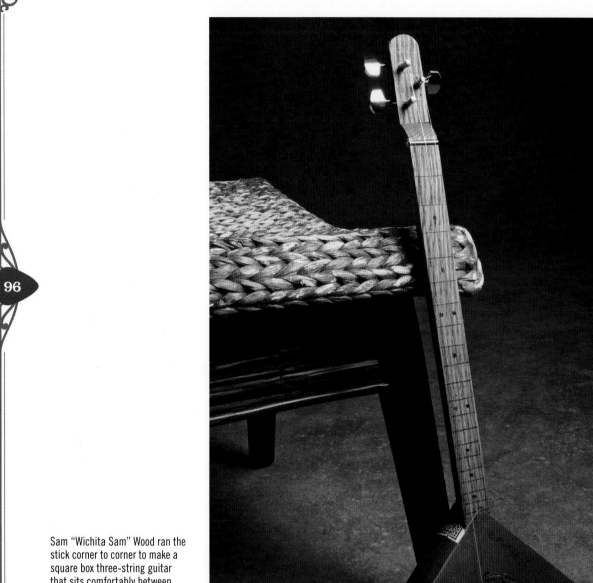

Sam "Wichita Sam" Wood ran the stick corner to corner to make a square box three-string guitar that sits comfortably between the player's knees.

TOP
Sam used picture hanging hardware to anchor the strings.

BOTTOM
This view shows how the neck is fitted into the corner of the square box.

TOP
Jerry Thompson, York,
Pennsylvania, 2010.

BOTTOM
Bill Jehle, Hunstville,
Alabama, 2010.

AN OBSESSION WITH CIGAR BOX GUITARS

Kevin Kraft, Kansas City,
Missouri, 2010.

RIGHT
The builder of this fretless five-string banjo from Lancaster, Pennsylvania, is unknown, as is its vintage. (From the collection of Bill Jehle.)

RIGHT
A detail photo shows the location of the fifth-string tuner.

ABOVE
A piece of tin has been used as a tailpiece/string anchor.

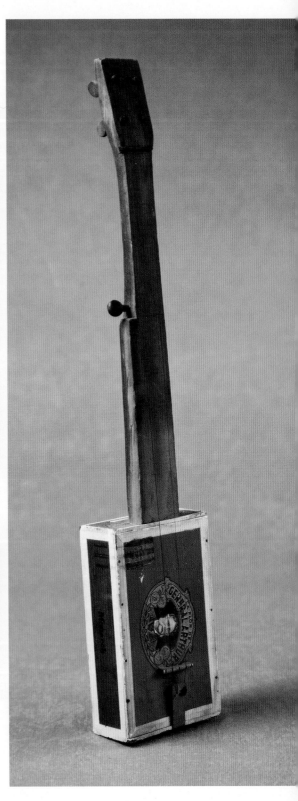

LEFT
Steampunk Victoria features Shawn Denman's handmade maple neck with an ebony-stained red-oak fretboard. He opted for jumbo nickel/silver frets and crafted position markers using cross-sections of a plastic chopstick. This six-string electric uses an EQ-7545R bar piezo pickup under the bridge.

ABOVE
Shawn salvaged gears from an old pocket watch to trick out *Steampunk Victoria*. These green LEDs draw on an internal 9-volt battery.

101

---◇---

LARRY FINE, "LARRY" OF THE THREE STOOGES

Fine was a master of the one-string cigar box violin during his pre-Stooges days in the Yiddish Vaudeville circuit. A classically trained violinist, Fine would entertain the crowds by bringing a crude-looking cigar box instrument on stage and perform standards on it. In fact, there was a tradition of using one-string cigar box violins in Vaudeville as a comedy prop. A former vaudevillian himself, W.C. Fields revived an old cigar box fiddle routine in his 1936 movie, *Poppy*. The comedy bit can be found with a quick search on YouTube for "W. C. Fields - Cigar Box Violin."

RIGHT
This San Cristobal three-string acoustic showed up while I was photographing guitars during the 2010 CBG Extravaganza in Huntsville, Alabama. Its builder is unknown. (From the collection of Bill Jehle.)

BELOW
The angled headstock was created with pocket-holes and screws.

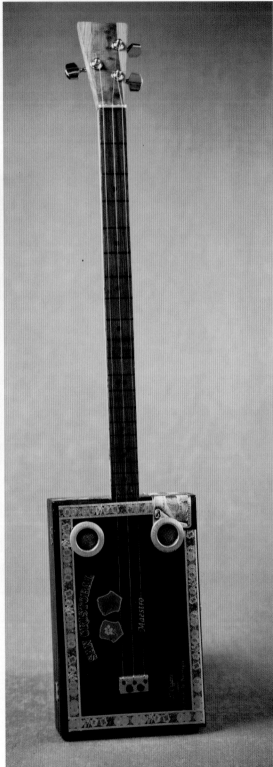

VINTAGE SPOTLIGHT

LEFT
This cigar box guitar by an unknown maker dates back to the 1940s and is thought to have been built in Wisconsin. It has remnants of cutouts from Captain Midnight comic books affixed to the top, which leads owner Bill Jehle to think it may have belonged to a child (Captain Midnight was a popular radio show in the '30s and '40s).

BELOW
Two whittled tuning pegs remain—the nut and third peg are lost to time.

RIGHT
Jeremiah Lee draws on art deco themes to turn his cigar box guitars into works of art. His instruments have been exhibited in several art galleries. This four-string fretted instrument is built around an asymmetrical cigar chest. Jeremiah uses paints, stains, dyes, and metalwork to embellish his guitars.

ABOVE
This photo offers a closer look at Jeremiah's work. Note how Jeremiah used paint and stain to emulate inlay in this fretboard.

RIGHT
In addition to carving his headstocks, Jeremiah often covers them with decorative metalwork.

ABOVE

This *Red Neck* guitar provided a lesson for me in where not to put a sound hole. With the instrument in playing position, the player's strumming hand blocks most of the sound. I added a pickup so it can be played through an amplifier.

LEFT

In my early explorations in headstock design, I tried creating more of a string break by gluing a piece of ¾" (2cm) poplar to the back of the neck (also ¾" [2cm] poplar), then shaping the joint. It worked, but it's not a strong joint. In fact, it broke while I was shaping it and had to be reglued. It has since held up nicely under all the use my nephew Michael has given it.

RIGHT
Here is a nicely crafted "split neck" guitar by John Nickel of Huntsville, Alabama. The guitar's two necks share a standard set of guitar strings, with the heavier/lower strings on the upper neck and the lighter/higher strings on the bottom neck. (From the collection of Bill Jehle.)

BELOW
Through-necks are laminated with oak flanked by black walnut. John "signs" his work by embedding nickels in his builds.

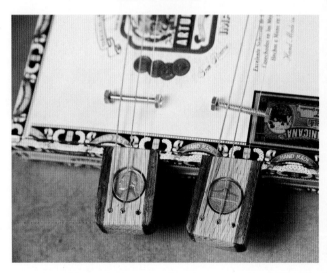

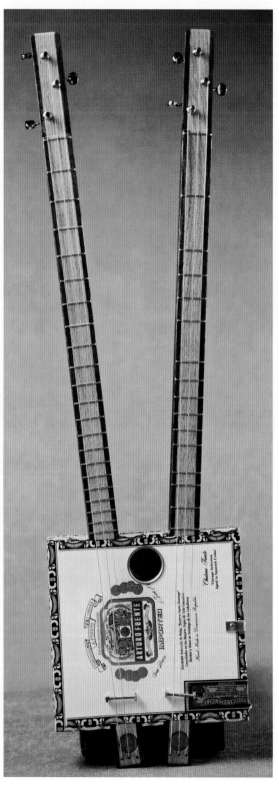

LEFT
This unusual KimmerO creation uses four strings and a diatonic scale. The short-scale neck is made from builder Kimmer Olesak's signature paduak.

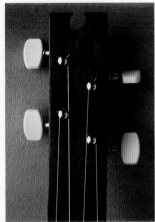

TOP
KimmerO favors the "zero fret," in which a piece of jumbo fret wire serves as the string nut.

BOTTOM
Adding a whimsical touch to this cigar box guitar, KimmerO built a spring-wound music box into his *Cuban Babies Music Box*. The music box plays "When You Wish Upon a Star."

To create the six-string electric, *Steampunk Elizabeth* guitar, Shawn Denman started with the neck from a First Act Strat copy he found at the Salvation Army. He fastened two Tabak Coffee Infused Cigar boxes together for the body, which lend this instrument a wonderful fragrance (Tabak cigars are soaked in coffee). He also used two pickups, accompanying electronics, and the bridge from the salvaged First Act guitar. What looks like a railroad spike on the right is actually half of a chrome shoe-horn. Shawn affixed the other half of the shoehorn to the copper pipe visible at left.

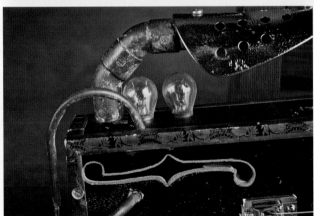

ABOVE

Other components of the guitar include a ½" (1.5cm) copper pipe, automobile tail light bulbs, compass body, and three F-holes trimmed with gold paint.

LEFT

While they won't light up literally, these retired light bulbs certainly light up the steampunk theme.

RIGHT
A "canjo" uses a tin can as a resonating chamber. This one, built by Glenn Kaiser, also uses a piezo buzzer as a pickup so that it can be played through an amplifier.

ABOVE LEFT
A long, thin bolt serves as a string nut for this electrified, two-string canjo.

ABOVE RIGHT
In an effort to demonstrate building a musical instrument from whatever you have, Glenn used eyebolts and wing nuts for tuners, drywall screws for string guides, and a cotter pin for a nut.

LEFT
Using a simple pine stick, an eyebolt, and a cookie tin, Glenn Kaiser built another playable three-stringed instrument from a Florentine cookie tin.

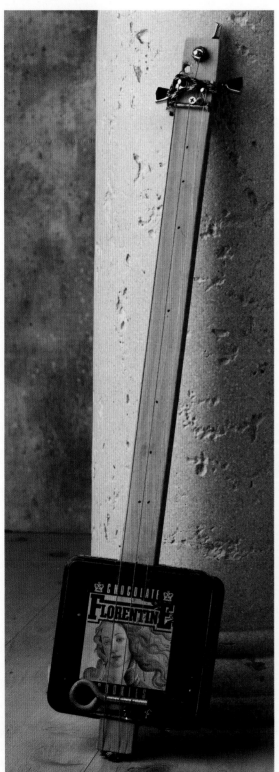

TOP
Salvaged guitar tuners finish off this cookie tin creation. Note how the builder has retro-fitted some screws as string guides.

BOTTOM
A detail shot shows the cookie tin used for Glenn's three-string guitar.

Reverend Gary Davis

"He told me that when he was a little kid, he used to
play a guitar someone had made for him out of
a cigar box, and there was this guy that used to come
through town who they called "the gittar man"—
that was the only name they knew him by.
He would come around once or twice a year, play in
the streets, and pick up some money and move on,
and 'Candyman' was a piece Gary learned from the gittar
man." (as told by guitar ace, Dave Van Ronk,
in his book *The Mayor of MacDougal Street*)

ABOVE
The tailpiece string anchor is
a model of simplicity.

RIGHT
Bill Jehle found this fully fretted cigar
box ukulele in a junk shop in Portland,
Maine, in the 1970s.

113

LEFT
This four-string electric was built by Rob "Hitone" Baker, a guitar maker and cigar box guitar maker whom Bill Jehle met through *projectguitar.com*. This guitar is equipped with a whammy bar fashioned out of cabinet hardware.

BELOW
Clever use of screw-eyes, threaded rod, and wing nuts create a bridge.

RIGHT

Splitting a set of six (three left/three right) tuners between two three-string guitars gave me the idea to make this pair—one fretted, one fretless—out of matching boxes. I cut the headstocks so they mirrored one another. Each has a piezo pickup under the bridge and a volume control knob. Some builders argue that the volume control isn't necessary with a piezo because the output is quite low. Piezos are notorious for feeding back, though, and I like to have a volume control to dial it down if things get out of control.

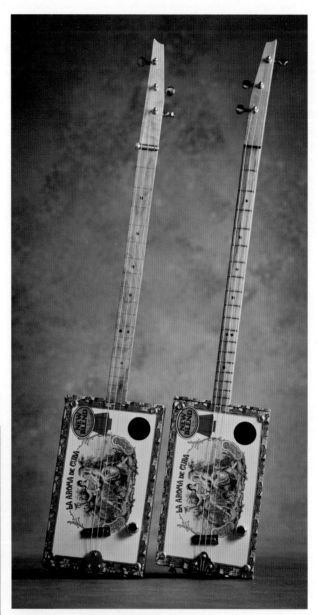

BELOW

I split a set of six tuners between the two guitars in this mirrored set of "sisters" guitars.

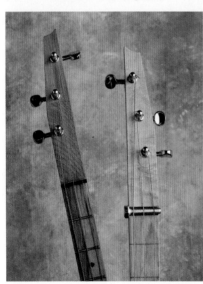

LEFT

The cigar boxes I chose each had a cigar overleaf with artwork that I used to decorate the insides of the boxes.

AN OBSESSION WITH CIGAR BOX GUITARS

115

LEFT
This instrument, made by John Lowe for blues musician Richard Johnston, combines a single string electric bass guitar on one neck with a three-string electric guitar on the other. The two instruments are played together with a slide. John uses his own hand-wound magnetic pickups to amplify the sound, and each neck (bass and guitar) has its own output jack. Shortly after it was built, Richard played this instrument (along with a high hat, snare, and kick drum) as a one-man band at the 2001 International Blues Challenge and won first prize in the international competition. He was also awarded the coveted Albert King Guitar Award.

BELOW
John had set the two necks so far apart on this first *Hill Harp* that Richard had to buy a 6" (15cm) piece of pipe from a plumbing supplier to use as a slide in order to cover all the strings.

VINTAGE SPOTLIGHT

RIGHT
This tiny cigar box guitar was apparently made for a child circa 1920 by an unknown builder and is owned by Bill Jehle. The builder cut a cigar box in half and made a miniature six-string instrument. It has hand-carved tuners and a very small neck.

ABOVE
Just three of the original hand-carved tuning pegs remain on this child's guitar.

LEFT
Diane Sutliff's innovative tuning dots enhance the user friendliness of her guitars. Starting with the heaviest string on this Padron three-string, you simply press the string down over the dot and tune the next string to match the pitch of the first string. Repeat the process by fretting the second string at the dot and tuning the third string to match pitch, and you're done.

BELOW
Diane adorned the sound hole of her Padron three-string with a salvaged broach, which complements the wood grain. The centered sound hole shows the through neck, so she decorated the neck with red fabric.

LEFT
David Williams, aka
"One String Willie",
plays his diddley
bow in Huntsville,
Alabama, 2010.

RIGHT
David plays in York,
Pennsylvania, 2010.

David strums on a cigar box guitar
in Hunstville, Alabama, 2010.

ABOVE
A close-up shot shows the detail of Tim Barnard's painting on the *Daddy Mojo Deluxe* model.

RIGHT
This Daddy Mojo issue four-string *Deluxe* model is hand painted by street artist Tim Barnard. It features a maple neck, rosewood fingerboard, and a high-gloss finish.

LEFT
A nicely crafted six-string "deco" electric cigar box guitar built by T. Stump and owned by Bill Jehle uses two hand wound magnetic pickups.

BELOW
Two pieces of matching Corian provide the string nut and tail guard. This headstock has been finished off with decorative wood extensions and a striking medallion.

121

ABOVE
For this kid's building project, Kevin used eyebolts as tuners and a thin bolt for a bridge.

RIGHT
Kevin Kraft helped his youngest daughter make this two-stringer from a discarded box.

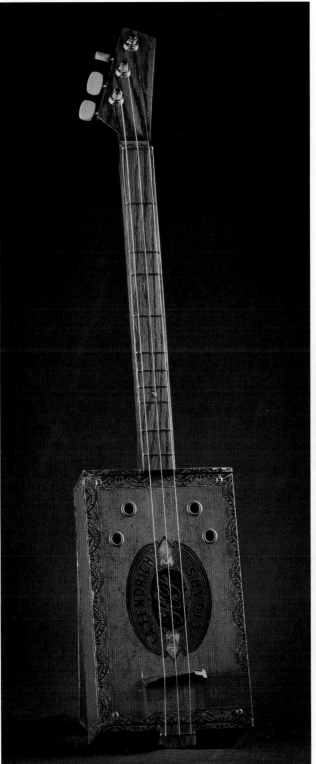

LEFT
Diane Sutliff built this La Fendrich three-string acoustic cigar box guitar around a diminutive antique cigar box.

BELOW
Diane prefers the "zero fret" to other string nut options. The zero fret is made by setting a piece of heavier (jumbo) fret wire in the nut position. She often uses three-on-a-plate tuners for her three-string acoustic builds. This oak neck has been attractively stained.

123

RIGHT
Brass, dye, and woodcarving all interplay in this three-stringer by Jeremiah Lee.

BELOW
Note how the shape of the wooden saddle is repeated in both the metalwork and the colored patterns.

BELOW
Pennsylvania builder David "One String Willie" Williams got things right on his first attempt at cigar box guitar building. He performs with this four-string, and as "One String Willie" with a single-string instrument called a diddley bow.

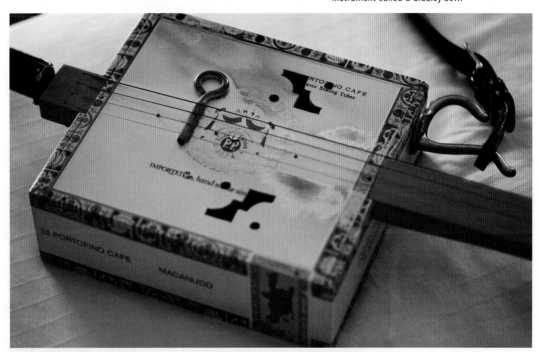

LEFT
David cut the headstock to match his guitar's sound holes.

RIGHT
Build #3 from my first book, *Cigar Box Guitars*, is a style some purists refer to as a "solid body electric guitar in a cigar box wrapper." But I always follow the first rule of cigar box guitar building: there are no rules. What a gas to be able to build and play your own electric guitar!

BELOW
A close-up photo shows the headstock with tuners and string tree.

ALBERT COLLINS

His first guitar was made from a cigar box: "People back in them days couldn't afford no guitar, man. I took a hay-baling wire and it was rough, man! You couldn't do nothing with it, so I just be banging it!"

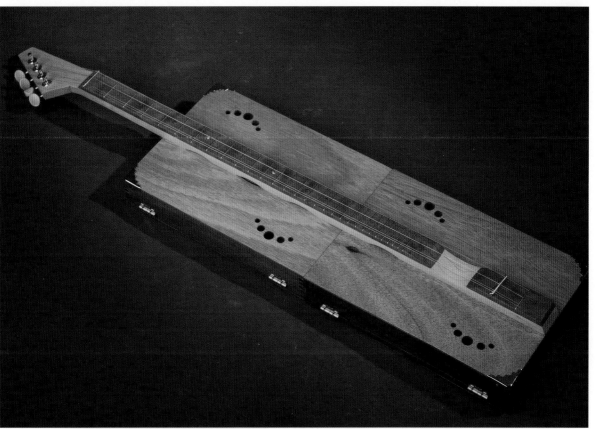

ABOVE

Diane Sutliff built this dulcimer by fastening two Padron boxes together. She uses the bottom of the boxes as her soundboard for dulcimers, because the wood is often thinner and has a nicer tonal quality. This four-string uses a doubled melody string and chromatic (guitar) fretting.

LEFT

Diane used cherry for the fretboard on top of a maple neck and brass rod for the bridge. She protects her fretboards from "string bite" by setting a piece of fret wire right next to the string holes.

RIGHT
This tin cigar box three-string guitar was
built by Al Hamilton. (From the collection
of Shane Speal).

BELOW
Al installed three-on-a-plate tuners
with the tuners facing forward.

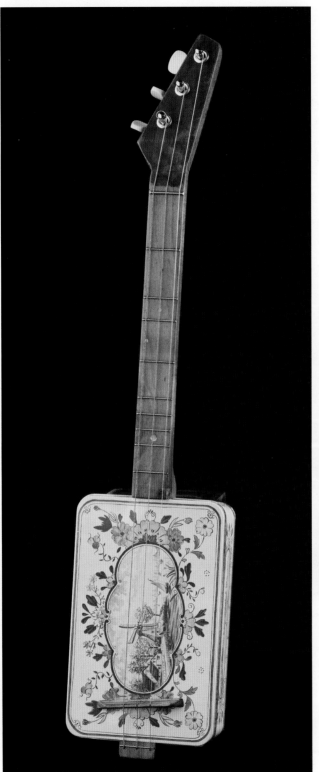

LEFT
This Delft Blauw cookie tin guitar by Diane Sutliff has a maple neck. A second board is glued under the first as a support for the part of the neck that has been thinned down to accept the lid.

BELOW
Diane glues two pieces of maple together to prevent the neck from warping under the tension of the strings.

TOP
Michael Ballerini built this combination harp/guitar to enter into one of Cigar Box Nation's occasional themed building contests—this one for double-necked guitars. Michael selected old-growth cherry milled more than fifty years ago for the guitar neck and harmonic curve.

BOTTOM
Michael's harp guitar combines a six-string guitar and six harp strings.

LEFT
This fretless four-string electric by Mike Orr uses spoons to form a string anchor, saddle, and faux whammy bar. Guitar labels and upholstery tacks make the position markers.

ABOVE
A detail shows the slotted spoons Mike used to make up the tailpiece and saddle. Note how wing nuts have been seated into the spoon's slots to support the bridge.

BELOW
Glenn Kaiser used a board-on-box
design for this thee-string guitar.

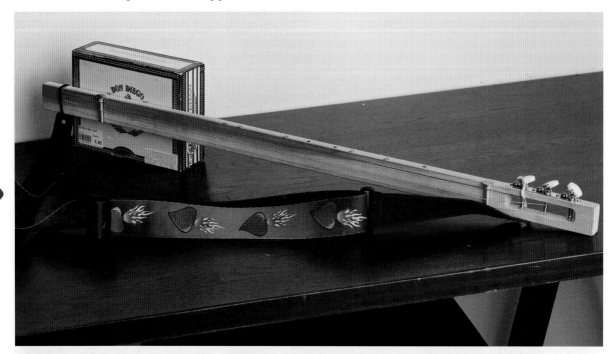

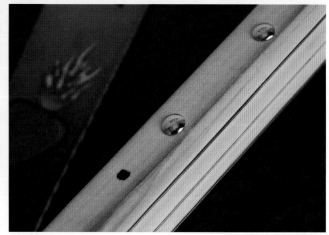

ABOVE LEFT
It uses a simple bolt as a string nut.

ABOVE RIGHT
Thumbtacks have been employed
as position markers.

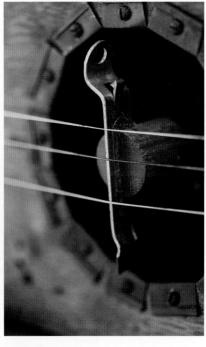

ABOVE
Paul fitted a can opener into a slot in an oak dowel to make the biscuit and bridge for this resonator guitar.

LEFT
Built by Paul Bessette of Uncle Pauly's Boxes, this three-string cigar box guitar has an oak neck with a carved headstock.

VINTAGE SPOTLIGHT

BELOW
This instrument by an unknown builder is best described as a cross between a guitar and a ukulele. Its four strings with a neck-through-body construction are reminiscent of a tenor banjo. (From the collection of Bill Jehle.)

BELOW
A close-up shows the hand-carved pine tuning pegs.

LEFT
The maker made ingenious use of wooden dowels to create the saddle/bridge.

BIG BILL BROONZY

Young Bill Broonzy first played music on a corn stalk
fiddle, eventually graduating to one made from
a cigar box. He got so good at playing the instrument
that the owner of the plantation he lived on invited
him to play at picnics and dances.

135

ABOVE
The *Daddy Mojo Standard Deluxe*
model with La Escepcion label
features four strings and one
mini-humbucker pickup.

LEFT
As demand for his Daddy Mojo
cigar box guitars increased, the
resourceful Lenny Piroth-Robert
contacted a cigar box manufacturer
in the Dominican Republic about
making standard-sized boxes to
order. This decision simplified
production and also enabled
Lenny to get his boxes imprinted
with the Daddy Mojo brand.
Pictured here is a *Daddy Mojo
Standard Deluxe* four-string
showing a DM branded box.

RIGHT

When Kevin Kraft went looking for cigar boxes to make his first cigar box guitar, the closest thing he could find was this silverware chest. He paid a dollar for it, and, using eyebolt tuners, built his first home-made guitar.

BELOW

Kevin used a brass hinge to reinforce the string holes and a bolt for a bridge.

ABOVE
Kevin used a woodburner to place position markers on the top side of his guitar neck, where they're easier to see.

LEFT
Kansas City guitar builder and blues musician Kevin Kraft used a heavy cotter pin for a bridge. Drain screens dress up the sound holes of this Cohiba three-string.

VINTAGE SPOTLIGHT

RIGHT
This is Bill Jehle's best example of an "Uncle Enos" banjo, built circa 1910. Daniel Carter Beard, cofounder of the Boy Scouts of America, published plans for a cigar box banjo in 1884 in *St. Nicholas Magazine* and later in his *American Boy's Handy Book*.

ABOVE
The painted headstock has been decorated with a cut-out picture of a rose.

ABOVE

A brass machine screw as a bridge rests atop an oak saddle. Diane fashioned the string anchor out of picture hanging hardware.

LEFT

Diane Sutliff used mandolin tuners and an oak neck with a 17" (43cm) scale for this four-string acoustic guitar. The third string is doubled with the fourth. This one has a brass theme: she used cross sections of brass rod for position markers and brass wire super-glued into the grooves for frets.

PHOTO BY MIKE LOWE

TOP
This four-string guitar/dulcimer with diatonic frets gets an acoustic boost from a 6" (15cm) "Lowecone"—a brass resonator cone that Mike spins himself.

BOTTOM
Mike Lowe built the biscuit (the wooden piece that sits atop the cone) for this guitar out of red oak and bois d'arc (osage orange). He added a nice decorative touch to the fretboard end as well.

PHOTO BY MIKE LOWE

BELOW
Kimmer Olesak built this guitar around an old cookie tin. It has a standard scale neck with diatonic fretting, and KimmerO used a piezo pickup for amplified playing.

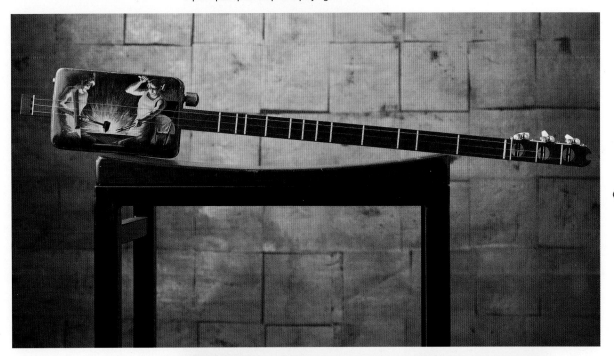

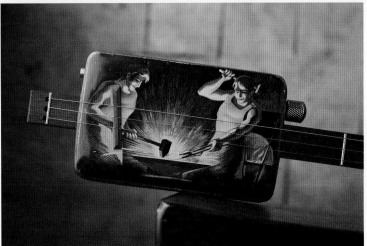

ABOVE
A silk-screened graphic adorns KimmerO's cookie tin guitar.

RIGHT
This beautifully crafted, modern, five-string banjo was built by an unknown maker around a Santa Clara cigar box. (From the collection of Bill Jehle.)

BELOW
The fifth-string tuner is mounted in a wooden block.

ABOVE
Richard has put more than a few miles on this John Lowe creation, with a lot of those musical miles spent busking on Beale Street in Memphis, Tennessee.

LEFT
The addition of two wooden wings to Richard Johnston's *Purgatory Hill Harp* by builder John Lowe makes this instrument reminiscent of a Gibson Flying V.

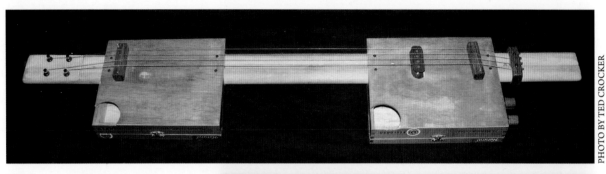

ABOVE
This four-string acoustic/electric lap guitar uses two cigar boxes and is designed by Ted Crocker to lie on the player's lap and be played lap steel style.

RIGHT
It is amplified by an original Ted Crocker hand-wound Stonehenge Pickup.

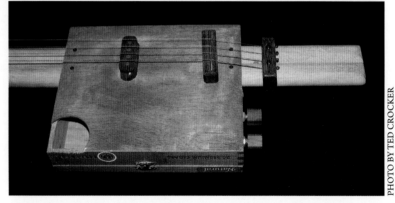

BLIND WILLIE JOHNSON

When Willie Johnson was just five years old, he told his father he wanted to preach the Gospel and play guitar when he grew up. To encourage his son, his father made him a one-string cigar box guitar using a simple stick-thru-box construction. Young Willie learned to play melodies up and down that lonely string using a pocketknife to fret the notes. This became essential training to his unique style of playing, for later on in life, he would incorporate the single string melodies on his six-string guitar. The best example of this is his phenomenal song "Dark Was The Night (Cold Was The Ground)." It should be noted that "Dark Was The Night" is one of the songs NASA chose for the golden record inside the Voyager Spacecraft. The song was chosen and championed by famed astronomer, Dr. Carl Sagan. Sagan commented, "Johnson's song concerns a situation he faced many times: nightfall with no place to sleep. Since humans appeared on Earth, the shroud of night has yet to fall without touching a man or woman in the same plight."

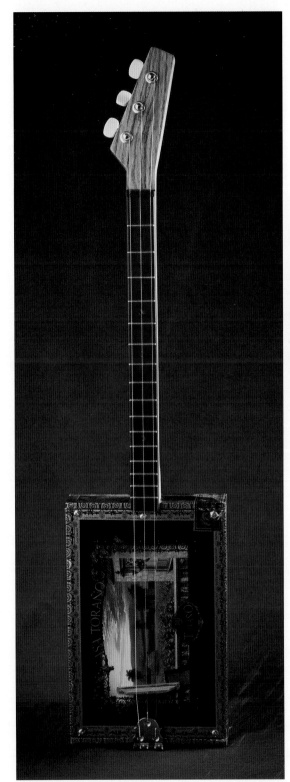

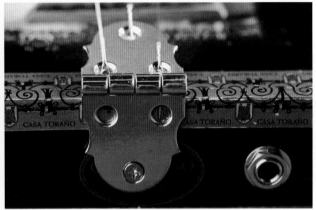

ABOVE
A heavy brass hinge provides a solid
string anchor.

LEFT
Diane Sutliff built this Casa Torano three-string
acoustic/piezo electric with a rosewood fretboard
over an oak neck. She's given it chromatic
(guitar) fretting.

LEFT

Kimmer Olesak crafted this three-string with diatonic fretting from an antique box. KimmerO favors padauk for necks, a wood that starts out orange and goes deep red with the application of an oil finish. This sweet sounding instrument also uses an upward facing sound hole, directing more sound to the player.

TOP

The sound hole is positioned to direct music to the player, suggesting an instrument designed for entertaining oneself.

BOTTOM

A detail of the artwork on the antique cigar box also shows the volume knob visible at the bottom left. This guitar is outfitted with a piezo pickup so it can be played through an amplifier.

ABOVE
A detail shows the double neck's sound holes.

LEFT
Darren Dukes' double-neck cigar box guitar combines a resonator four-string with an acoustic four-string. (From the collection of Shane Speal.)

ABOVE
Kurt Schoen is the builder of this three-string resonator guitar. (From the collection of Shane Speal.)

RIGHT
A detail of the brass tailpiece on Kurt's guitar shows the etched autograph.

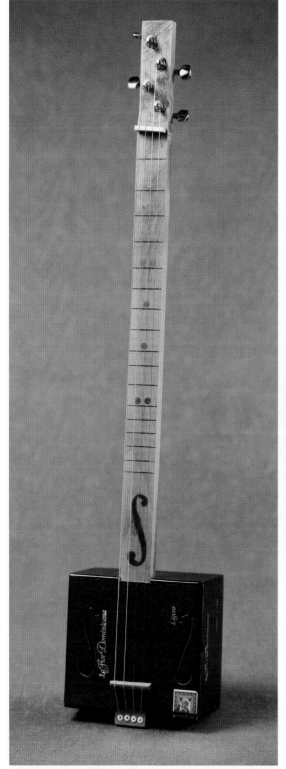

LEFT
The unknown builder used a red marker to indicate fret lines and decorate the fretboard on this La Flor four-string fretless guitar and made nice use of S-shaped sound holes. (From the collection of Bill Jehle.)

BELOW
This bridge looks like it might be Corian, a material that can be worked with woodworking tools but has a nice density for conducting sound vibrations.

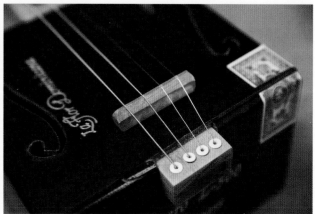

LEFT
This six-string electric has a maple neck and rosewood fingerboard. Known as the *Daddy Mojo Dolorosa* model, it is adorned with a silk-screened sacred heart design.

ABOVE
A detail shot shows the sacred heart design on Lenny Piroth-Robert's *Daddy Mojo Dolorosa*.

ABOUT THE AUTHOR

PHOTO BY MARC HAUSER.

During his three decades as a professional photographer, David Sutton has always managed to steal time for handiwork. Whether restoring old hand tools, carving wood, making jewelry, or, of course, building cigar box guitars, he has always found something valuable in working with his hands that couldn't be replaced by his more practical pursuits. Coming from a long line of teachers and tradesmen, perhaps it was inevitable that David would write a book showing people how to build something.

So it was that his first book, *Cigar Box Guitars*, appeared in 2012 to wide acclaim. His years of research on the topic introduced him to and incorporated him into the stimulating world of cigar box guitars, a world rich with art, music, community and meaning.

What better person than this gifted photographer to write a book about the beauty of cigar box guitars,

and the passion—the obsession—builders and players feel for their craft, their instruments and their culture? David is a keen observer who uses his talents as a photographer to document the guitars; he's a reporter who has studied and greatly respects the roots of the craft; and he is a builder who has himself successfully built many guitars. David's even a player who loves to sing along with his strumming.

In his other life, David operates Sutton Studios, a high-end portrait studio in Evanston, Illinois. He specializes in an artful and humorous approach to photographing dogs and cats and the people they inevitably bring to the studio with them. He thinks of it as relationship portraiture (*suttonstudios.com*).

David also enjoys Sutton Studios' charitable efforts, which have helped raise over a million dollars for dozens of animal and human welfare organizations over the last twenty years.

ACKNOWLEDGMENTS

The author would like to thank the following artists for their time, their dedication to the craft, and their willingness to share their work by contributing to this book. The growing, thriving world of cigar box guitars is truly the result of the efforts of people like these.

David Williams aka One String Willie. David Williams has been learning to play guitar since his fifteenth birthday. He discovered cigar box guitars in 2004, made his first diddley bow in 2006, and made his first public appearance as One String Willie in 2007. The diddley bow has been his main instrument since that time, and he continues to enjoy teaching himself to play it. A research scientist, he works in Bethesda, Maryland, and lives with his wife, Miz Charlotte, and their herd of cats in Tylersport, Pennsylvania. *onestringwillie.com*

Diane Sutliff. Diane Sutliff wants everybody to make music, and she designs and builds instruments to make music making more accessible to the non-musically inclined. She lives in Chicago and teaches art to students in the Chicago Public Schools. She has small hands. *chicagocbg.blogspot.com*

John Lowe. From the back room of his Memphis, Tennessee, store, Xanadu Music and Books, innovator John Lowe designs and builds musical instruments, many built around cigar boxes. He likes oak dowels, his own hand-wound pickups, and feedback. Lowe also steps out musically as a one-man band. *myspace.com/johnnylowebow*

Kevin Kraft. Kevin Kraft lives in Kansas City, Missouri, where he is the driving force behind the annual Kansas City Cigar Box Guitar Festival. Kraft also gives inspirational talks around the construction of a diddley bow. *kevinmkraft.weebly.com*

Lenny Piroth-Robert. Operating as Daddy Mojo Guitars, Montreal artist and entrepreneur Lenny Piroth-Robert skillfully walks that fine line between artistry and mass production. Innovation, invention, and staying hands-on have kept him and his hand-built instruments safe from the dark side. *daddy-mojo.com*

153

Mike Orr. Mike Orr is a professional carpenter and owner of Built2Last Guitars. He has designed, built, and sold hundreds of instruments. The highlight of his career was when guitar legend Robert Randolph played one of his guitars in front of a live audience. When he is not in the shop, Mike can usually be found touring the music festival circuit in his VW van, where he demonstrates and leads classes on building cigar box guitars. *built2lastcigarboxguitars.webs.com*

Shane Speal. Shane Speal lives and works in York, Pennsylvania. He's a full-time cigar box guitar professional, performing constantly, building and innovating daily. He's also a spirited advocate for this humble instrument and for anyone interested in finding his or her own voice. Read about Speal in the introduction to this book and in Cigar Box Guitars, also by this author/publisher. *shanespeal.com*

Shawn Denman. Shawn Denman, a "small town boy" living in the big city of Chicago, rocks the steampunk and still feels the magic every time he strings a new guitar and hears its music for the first time. *facebook.com/shawn.denman*

Bill Jehle. Alabama native Bill Jehle wanted to build the perfect electric guitar for recording his music. His quest led him, instead, to making cigar box guitars from junk. Now fronting his cigar-box-guitar-based Nadaband from Decatur, Alabama, Jehle thinks having 100 strange-looking instruments—his Cigar Box Guitar Museum collection—and too many gigs is far better than having one perfect guitar and no career. *bellyjellymusic.com*

Brian Romero aka Bairfoot Cajun. Brian Romero calls himself "an educated Cajun from the swamps of Louisiana." Romero currently lives on the Cumberland Plateau in middle Tennessee. He has been called a pioneer and innovator of cigar box guitar designs. *cigarboxnation.com/profile/brianromero*

John McNair. Originally from New Orleans, John McNair grew up absorbing that gumbo of music and culture that "can be found nowhere else in the world." He has been playing and building homemade guitars since he was 14. Now living in Puerto Rico, John remains proud that his birthplace is also the birthplace of Jazz and Blues. *reddogguitars.com*

Glenn Kaiser. Glenn Kaiser is a Chicago-based blues musician, singer-songwriter and pastor. With Rez Band, Glenn Kaiser Band, and solo projects he has recorded 40 full-length albums to date. Cigar box and found-object guitars have lately become his passion. *grrrrecords.com/glennkaiser.cfm*

Josh Gayou. Josh Gayou operates Smokehouse Guitars, a small, one-man custom guitar shop in Lake Elsinore, California. Josh was first bitten by the CBG bug in 2008, and has been making custom guitars for musicians and enthusiasts since. *smokehouseguitars.com*

Ted Crocker. Ted Crocker hosts the Handmade Music Clubhouse social network (*handmademusicclubhouse.com*), where he's been helping people online, on the phone, and in person daily since 2003. Crocker created guitars for the Danny Glover movie Honeydripper, and Keith Urban currently plays a Crocker onstage. Crocker's hand-crafted pickups are in thousands of cigar box and custom guitars worldwide. *tedcrocker.com*

Al Hamilton. Al Hamilton enjoys having people ask him where he got the guitar he's playing, because he gets to answer, "I didn't buy it, I built it." Originally inspired by one of Shane Speal's videos, Hamilton has built over 300 guitars in his Snow Shoe, Pennsylvania shop. *facebook.com/al.hamilton.520*

155

Darren Brown. Darren Brown calls the seaside village of Canning, Nova Scotia home. He has worked as a carpenter and finish carpenter for thirty years, and he's been playing and repairing guitars for just as long. Darren was bitten by the cigar box guitar bug in about 2001. *dbrowncustoms.blogspot.com*

Darren Dukes. Operating as Delta Groove Guitars since 2008, Darren "Big Daddy" Dukes and his brother Dan have sent cigar box guitars, kits, necks, and parts "all over the globe." They're spreading the CBG gospel from their Irvington, Illinois shop "one neck at a time."

That's Jimbo Mathus in the photo with them. [L to R: Darren, Jimbo, Dan] *cigarboxnation.com/profile/DeltaGrooveGuitars*

Kurt Schoen. Retired Air Force pilot Kurt Schoen lives in Walla Walla, Washington. He has background in drawing, painting, aircraft tooling, and manufacture and aeronautical engineering, and he has a day job flying cargo planes. Schoen started building cigar box guitars in 2001 to entertain his then-small children. He now builds a wide variety of stringed instruments. *schoenguitars.com*

Lloyd "MadMan" Madansky. Lloyd "MadMan" Madansky has been making cigar box guitars since 2003. He builds them in his home workshop in Arroyo Grande, California, and sells them locally at art fairs and music festivals. He also conducts workshops on building CBGs for kids of all ages. *cigarboxnation.com/profile/LloydMadManMadansky*

Michael Ballerini. Michael Ballerini lives just outside Detroit in Clawson, Michigan, and says that building Cigar Box Guitars calms him right down. When he's not building cigar box guitars he can be found selling them (his, and some built by others!) on weekends at the Rust Belt Marketplace in Ferndale, Michigan.

Paul "Uncle Pauly" Bessette. Paul Bessette, award-winning tattoo artist and purveyor of Uncle Pauly's Boxes, grew up on Long Island, on or near the water pretty much all the time. He sings sea shanties. He got into cigar box guitars because he wanted to accompany his own singing and found six strings unmanageable. He's been a percussionist for over four decades. He thinks everyone should sing. *unclepaulyart.com*

Matty Baratto. Hollywood is home for Matty Baratto, who has been a professional luthier since 1993. He started building cigar box guitars in 1994, and his Cigfiddles have been seen in the hands of such luminaries as Paul McCartney, Johnny Depp, and Steven Tyler.

Baratto has made over 250 cigar box guitars and he's proud to point out that his Cigfiddles can also be heard on several records: Alain Johannes' "Spark," PJ Harvey's "White Chalk," and Brody Dalle's "Spinnerette," to name a few.

Baratto is living his dream, and if you have one, he thinks you should live yours, too. *barattoguitars.com*

Peter Seman. Peter Seman played fiddle professionally with bluegrass and Texas swing bands for 10 years in Buffalo, New York before moving to Chicago to attend the Chicago School of Violin Making, from which he graduated in 1988. He now operates Seman Violins in Skokie, Illinois, where he's currently working on violins patterned after Stradivari and Guarneri, and cellos and violas patterned after Stradivari. *semanviolins.com*

Jeremiah Lee. With a background in metal smithing and fine woodworking, Jeremiah Lee builds guitars inspired by depression era art and design movements. He lives and works in Chicago, a city with a handful of exceptional CBG builders and a tremendous DIY spirit. Lee loves the history of the CBG and he's a terrible musician.

157

John Nickel. John Nickel hails from Florence, Alabama, home of the W.C. Handy Blues Festival. He saw Microwave Dave Gallaher playing a cigar box guitar at the Handy, and immediately knew where he was headed. Well, sort of. Whether he knew he'd soon be operating what he calls the world's first cigar box guitar store (Nickel CBGs) out of a repurposed shoe mill in Huntsville, Alabama is open to debate, but that's where you'll find him.

Kimmer Olesak. Kimmer Olesak spent many good hours in detention at Jack Benny Jr. High School in Waukegan, Illinois. So it seemed fitting that they should appoint the class clown to be Jack Benny's guide on one of the comedian's visits to his hometown. Today Olesak (better known as KimmerO) works as a cameraman, shooting for television and film. He says he's a big fan of cigar box guitars as folk art, and he is so moved that other people can actually produce music from the instruments he builds from discarded materials that he often just gives them away.
cigarboxnation.com/profile/KimmerOlesak

INDEX

All famous player facts courtesy of Shane Speal. Fact credits: page 21, *Guitar Player* Magazine, 1976; page 33, *Pittsburgh Post Gazette*; page 43, *Guitar Player* Magazine; page 83, *Guitar Player* interview with Robert Lockwood Jr., July 1991, Journalist, Peter Lee; page 89, *nps.gov/history*; page 126, *Guitar Player* Magazine, July 1993; page 144, Sagan quote from Nelson, Stephanie and Larry Polansky, "The Music of the Voyager Interstellar Record," Journal of Applied Communication Research (November 1993).

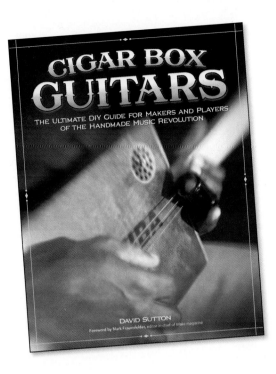

Cigar Box Guitars
*The Ultimate DIY Guide for Makers and Players
of the Handmade Music Revolution*
By DAVID SUTTON

More than just a how-to guide, this book chronicles the modern revival of the cigar box guitar. You'll learn a bit about its roots, influential personalities, and the cultural trends that are bringing this instrument back to the musical landscape. Author and professional photographer David Sutton introduces readers to the faces of the CBG movement with in-depth profiles and photographic portraits of fascinating builders and performers. Here is a perfect opportunity to put a real American tradition in your own hands.

ISBN 978-1-56523-547-2 **$29.95**

Handmade Music Factory
*The Ultimate Guide to Making
Foot-Stompin' Good Instruments*
By MIKE ORR

Hand-making musical instruments is part of a growing trend that even celebrities such as guitar legend Jack White are taking part in. It doesn't require a lot of money or an expertise in woodworking and electronics—all it takes is a little creativity.

In *Handmade Music Factory*, handyman Mike Orr guides you through the construction of eight of the most unique and imaginative instruments found anywhere—from a one-string guitar made from a soup can, to a hubcap banjo, to a stand-up lap steel guitar made from a vintage ironing board. There are also directions for an amp that can be assembled using inexpensive parts from the local electronics store. There's no shortage of inspiration to draw upon in creating an arsenal of instruments that look good, sound great, and deliver some foot stompin' fun!

ISBN 978-1-56523-559-5 **$22.95**

More Great Books from Fox Chapel Publishing

Learn to Play the Ukulele
ISBN 978-1-56523-687-5 **$14.95**

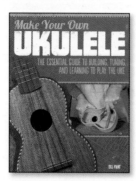

Make Your Own Ukulele
ISBN 978-1-56523-565-6 **$17.95**

Wood Pallet Projects
ISBN 978-1-56523-544-1 **$19.99**

Learn to Burn
ISBN 978-1-56523-728-5 **$16.99**

**The Art of Steampunk,
Revised Second Edition**
ISBN 978-1-56523-785-8 **$19.99**

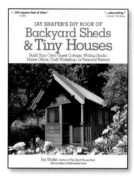

**Jay Shafer's DIY Book of
Backyard Sheds & Tiny Houses**
ISBN 978-1-56523-816-9 **$19.99**

WOODCARVING ILLUSTRATED **SCROLL SAW woodworking** & CRAFTS

In addition to being a leading source of woodworking books and DVDs, Fox Chapel also publishes two premiere magazines. Released quarterly, each delivers premium projects, expert tips and techniques from today's finest woodworking artists, and in-depth information about the latest tools, equipment, and materials.

Subscribe Today!

Woodcarving Illustrated: **888-506-6630**
Scroll Saw Woodworking & Crafts: **888-840-8590**
www.FoxChapelPublishing.com

Look for These Books at Your Local Bookstore or Specialty Retailer or at *www.FoxChapelPublishing.com*